Improve Your Emotional Intelligence:

The Spiritual Development of Your Emotions

The Enlightenment Series Volume 2

ELSABE SMIT

Contents

Contents

When you see this symbol throughout the book, pause and reflect. Make notes, answer the question or complete the exercise.

1 A BAD HAIR DAY

When we wake up in the morning, we all look like a version of the devil in the children's bible, with hair standing in all directions. We then choose how to approach the day, and if we make the wrong choice, we have a 'bad hair day'. Is that fair on our hair? And some young people (and people who want to believe they are still young) spend a fortune on hair gel and cultivating that porcupine look that the rest of us try to get rid of before we leave the house.

We all feel less than great at times. Of course, there is the 'bad hair day', which friends can commiserate with because, like you, they know this is nothing serious. It really is a cry for a friend to go with you to buy another pair of shoes or a pint of beer, whichever way you are inclined. You recognize these people because one talks all the time and the other one only says knowingly "I know . . . Isn't it just . . . I know . . . Of course, not . . . "and so on. We all need that from time to time. I have a client who only calls me about twice a year. When she calls, I know it is so that I can listen to her tales and tell her she is a great person.

Then there are the days when we simply choose to feel like whining about things, especially the weather and the government. (Why on earth does everyone the world over have such an obsession with the weather?) When we choose to have a miserable day, the worst we can encounter is someone who is radiant with happiness, because it somehow tells us we are wrong, and that makes our day worse.

 When was the last time you woke up out of sorts and your day just got worse? How did you manage it?

Of course, we can consciously choose to change our mood. It does take some effort, like finding your direction again when you get lost in a city you do not know. You can continue to just drive until you leave the city, and then retrace your steps to get to your destination, or you can focus on driving to the end of the one-way street, and then use your inner compass to go into the right direction and be on your way again.

If you feel like whining and complaining but choose to rather jump up and down, do a few war cries and take a few deep breaths, you will immediately pop out of the whining mood, because you will simply have too much energy to hang your shoulders and your face. You may get a few funny looks in the office, but at least you will feel much better for the rest of the day – and get a laugh out of other whining people which will make them feel better. Try it – it works.

Of course, laughing also raises your vibrations. It does not matter whether it is a giggle by yourself or a deep laugh that comes from your stomach.

You do not need to laugh at a good joke. All you need to do is laugh, and notice how your emotions change. There are companies that have tried this – a laughing session to start the day – and it improved their productivity.

They did not allow any jokes – at some point you could either run out of jokes or offend someone - and people's sense of humor differ anyway. Laughing works all the time if you want to raise the energy in a room, and it is contagious.

There is also the darkness that we experience after an incident, like a divorce or an accident. Some people experience it and then decide to move on (this takes time, but we all have our incidents and it is possible to accept them as part of our life path and then move on).

 How do you define yourself? If you are not happy with your answer, how can you change that definition and then be happy with the person you see in the mirror?

Other people define themselves in terms of that incident for the rest of their lives, and often join organizations that make them feel like traitors if they choose to move on. I am referring to organizations that help people "recover" from alcoholism or rape or losing a child and so on. I am sure they initially do good work, but the survival of the organization depends on having dedicated members – people who choose to relive their experiences for a long time rather than integrate the experiences and get on with their lives.

If you are simply having a bad hair day, trust me, nothing beats retail therapy. Just don't buy any clothes when you are in such a mood, because when you feel better and you see what you have spent your money on, you will get yourself into a mother of a depression.

2 A SHATTERED RELATIONSHIP

There are few life events that are as life-shattering as ending a long-term relationship, whether it is a divorce or widowhood or a decision to part ways without any contractual ties.

Dealing with the practical arrangements, for example a funeral, dividing property or settling for child maintenance, and the paperwork related to the split, are often the easy parts. However, even these actions can add to the immense turmoil of emotions that suddenly explode when a beloved partner is no longer there for you.

If the partner was not necessarily beloved and there is the additional trauma of an abusive relationship that has suddenly ended, it is no wonder that some people become unable to function and do even the simplest things.

Many recently single people are at first unaware of the immense anger that they radiate. They like to believe that their friends avoid them because the friends do not understand or no longer want them as friends.

 Have you ever felt or noticed this anger about a separation?

But consider this: have you ever been introduced to a person and immediately felt - for no good reason - that you do not want to be in the presence of this person? Have you ever seen someone for example on television – a person that you have never even met – and had a similar reaction to this stranger? This is an intuitive and illogical response that is often later justified (at least in your own mind) when you receive more information about the person.

People tend to intuitively have a similar response to grieving people. I say similar, because when you meet a person that is shattered by grief and struggling to keep themselves together for even the simplest task, you do not necessarily dislike them – on the contrary.

You rather feel their immense pain and confusion of the grieving person at an unconscious level. You also intuitively observe the aura of the grieving person – and you do this regardless of your belief that you are not able to 'see' auras.

 How do you normally deal with grief – your own or someone else's?

If you have had similar experiences in the past and managed to work through your own experiences, you will be able to respond intuitively in your own way. You will be able to acknowledge and neutralize some of the anger of your friend – for the moment, because such deep anger does not get resolved in the blink of an eye.

If you have not had any experience that will give you even an inkling of the deep emotions your friend is experiencing, you have choices on how to deal with this change in your friendship.

The first option is simply to walk away. Many people do that and miss out on an opportunity for self-growth. They also leave their friend in a space that confirms their sense of isolation and loneliness.

The second option is to continue as if nothing much has changed, and not to acknowledge the strong emotions of your friend. This is probably worse than walking away, because you deny your own emotions and you deny the change in the friendship.

 Are you ready to go back to someone whose grief you denied? Even if it is only to have a conversation with that person in your mind?

The third option is to understand that everything happens for a reason, and that this friendship is part of your life path. For goodness sake, do not tell your friend that the relationship ended for a reason – they will discover that in their own time. When you tell them this while they are so full of strong emotions such as anger, telling them that there is a reason for their immense pain would be proof that you just don't understand.

Rather use the opportunity to say to your friend 'I want to walk this path with you, but have no idea what to do to help. Please tell me how I can help.'

Be prepared for every reaction from 'Leave me alone' to 'Be with me all the time'. Be prepared for using your common sense and doing practical things like mowing the lawn or offering to baby-sit. Be prepared for observing lots of crying and knowing that you cannot take the pain away, and learn to take it in your stride and remain a friend. Be prepared for remaining a friend and growing in the process.

Above all, be prepared for loving your friend no matter what.

What can you do today to practically make life easier for someone else?

3 VEGAN FRIENDS

"I didn't know it was made from butter" I said apologetically.

Josiah gave me a withering look. I suddenly felt cold and wanted to leave the room. Of course, that would mean leaving Marie with him.

For a split-second Marie pleaded with her eyes and I understood. I also understood the bruises on her upper arms. She had tried to hide them earlier on in the bathroom, then told me that she was iron-deficient and bruised easily. In all the years that I had known her, she had never been ill.

Josiah pushed his plate away. "Would you like a clean plate?" I asked. "I am quite sure all the other dishes are vegan."

"No." he abruptly pushed his chair back and gave Marie an order with his eyes. "Please excuse us," she whimpered softly. Everybody heard her because the room had gone quiet.

"I am sorry, we have to go," Josiah said. He looked at me. "We will be in touch" he said. A vision of a black crow crossed my mind and I suppressed a shudder.

I wanted to jump up and pull Marie back. I now understood why we were no longer best friends - why she always had an excuse not to visit me. I understood why she insisted on having a vegan meal if she and Josiah were to accept our invitation for dinner. I had thought that she was so in love and wanted to impress us with her new husband and his vegan lifestyle.

This dinner was my final attempt to revive my and Marie's childhood friendship.

I was surprised when she called me. She told me that they would be in town and on the spur of the moment I invited them to dinner. When we spoke on the phone she described his strong character, his drive, his way with people. He sounded quite impressive.

The morning after the dinner I called Marie. I could hear the tension in her voice and that scared me. Dear Marie was always like a butterfly, gentle and flighty. Now she was like a moth being drawn to a candle. I wanted to get her away from the candle.

"Marie," I said, "Remember that I am always here for you. Please talk to me and let me help you."

"I don't know what you are talking about. Thank you for the meal last night. I am sorry we had to leave so soon, but Josiah has an important business meeting this morning. I will call you when we are in town again. Good bye."

I started crying. We had had such a lovely friendship. I did not know it was made of butter.

 Have you ever judged another person only to discover that you were unfair? Looking back, how did you change your thinking after you discovered your mistake?

4 CAN WE HEAL THE WORLD WITH LOVE?

Which is more important - justice or mercy? The more emotional the issue, the more divided the opinions. We often encounter issues that tempt us to decide: should we insist on justice, knowing that justice always have consequences? Should we show mercy and always try and understand the other side of the coin? Or should public opinion be the determining factor?

In recent years, several these emotional issues have been in the headlines.

Burma's military regime jailed and charged the pro-democracy opposition leader, Aung San Suu Kyi, because a man swam across a lake to her house. She was accused of violating the terms of her house arrest and faced a possible sentence of five years in prison. She has been confined to her house for at least 13 of the past 19 years. Is that not a form of imprisonment as well? So, the fuss was not about her being in prison. It was about her exchanging one kind of prison for another without having any say in the matter because she stands for democracy. And where was the justice in punishing her for the actions of another person?

But could there possibly be another side to this argument? She was probably charged under the Safeguarding the State from the Dangers of the Subversive Elements law in Burma. There are people in Burma who do not want complete democracy. There is a culture in Burma which suits the Burmese people, and they regard democracy as subversive and as a threat to their culture.

Are the Burmese people entitled to take such a stance? Surely, they have freedom to choose against democracy as much as they have freedom to choose for democracy? If democracy works in one country, how can we assume that it is suitable for every other country?

South Africa, a country that is known for its hospitality and Ubuntu (love for your neighbor) was in the news for having no mercy for their

9

neighbors.

Many Zimbabwean citizens have entered South Africa illegally. The health system in Zimbabwe has collapsed completely, and there is hardly any food for the citizens. On the other hand, conditions in South Africa are in general far better than in Zimbabwe.

The overloaded health system in South Africa is already under pressure because of the high incidence of HIV/AIDS and the population growth.

South Africa has less than 7 doctors per 10 000 people whereas the UK has around 21, the United States around 24 and many European countries more than 30. More than 60% of the medical doctors who choose to stay in South Africa serve less than 20% of the population.

South Africa got criticized for failing to provide health services to Zimbabwean citizens that are illegally in South Africa. These people are unable to pay for their food, let alone any medical service. Should the South African government provide for Zimbabweans who are suffering because of an insane dictatorship, or should they look after their own tax-paying citizens first and ignore the plight of these old, frail illegal immigrants?

The closure of Guantanamo Bay was heralded by some, and questioned by others. The inmates of Guantanamo Bay had been accused of horrendous crimes against humanity and tortured for these crimes. Is torture justified when it is done on behalf of a government, but not justified when the opposition to the government become the torturers? A terrorist and a freedom fighter are defined by one's perspective.

It is interesting to see how many of the opponents of Guantanamo Bay were unwilling to accept the prisoners that were released from the camp. Was this really a matter of "we only look after our own", or is it a matter of "not in my back yard, even if it is my own"? On what grounds, could the countries that protested the imprisonment and torture of people have refused to provide refuge to those same prisoners?

 What great injustice touches your heart? Have you ever thought of showing mercy to the perpetrators?

This reminds us of the legal action against Nazi war criminals. Yes, atrocities were committed by these people. But how just is retributive action now when it is taken against a sickly octogenarian who must be uprooted from the country where he has lived for over 50 years so that he can die in prison? Where is the mercy in that? Surely such people have had to live with their consciences all these years.

People donated money to World Vision, only to discover that more than $1 million of the donations never reached Liberia because of fraud. Is it such a good idea to give money to charitable organizations, especially when the donations are solicited by means of expensive television ads and uniquely labeled free pens to sign the donation slips with? Or should we support these international charities knowing that some of the money they receive does make a difference? How much worse off would the recipients of this charity be if there was no charity organization?

The Chinese government banned Hotmail, Twitter and Flickr on the anniversary of the Tiananmen Square massacre. There will be people in China who applaud this move because they understand the immense damage that the media can do when they get hold of a story and blow it out of proportion – we see that all the time with a celebrity culture in the Western world.

There will similarly be people who will object to their freedom of thought and free speech being taken away from them. Is there ever a reason that is good enough to prevent people from accessing information so that they can read and decide for themselves what is right?

The Justice card in tarot reminds us that whenever we look for justice, we should be aware of the consequences. We should open our hearts to our fellow human beings and understand that we are Love above all. Justice can never be applied without mercy.

 Have you ever judged another person because their actions are so heinous that you cannot forgive them? What if you must forgive them so that you can grow and gain wisdom?

Is it possible that Love alone can provide answers to all these issues?

Dr. Joe Vitale, in his book *Zero Limits*, describes a Hawaiian healing process called ho'oponopono. The therapist who made this healing process famous was put in charge of a ward of criminally insane patients. This was a ward where psychologists quit routinely and staff either called in sick very often, or simply quit their jobs.

This therapist never saw any of the patients. He simply went through their files every day, and then looked within himself to see how he created that person's illness. The therapist then repeated "I am sorry, I love you". As he learnt to love the parts of himself that he earlier did not want to acknowledge, the patients improved significantly. Some patients were released, others were taken off heavy medication, and others were allowed to move around without shackles.

This method of therapy was so successful that eventually there were more (happy) staff members than patients, and today that ward is closed. This is not an urban legend. It was confirmed by the therapist, Dr. Ihaleakala Hew Len, who is the co-author of the book.

What if we do not try to find existential or practical or morally right answers to any of the questions raised in this article? What if we simply try this method of ho'oponopono to love ourselves, rather than take part in the debate about issues that we can never resolve by debate?

Is ho'oponopono the ultimate combination of justice and mercy?

And if healing the world with Love sounds like a pipe dream - have you heard about the hugging judge? Lee Shapiro was a retired judge, living in San Francisco. He was a very popular speaker at conferences, where he delivered his message of unconditional love.

At a conference, he was challenged by the media to prove his message. The first challenge was simply to approach any person in the street and offer a hug. When that proved easy, he was told to approach a meter maid who was having a hard time with an offender. She gratefully accepted his hug, to the chagrin of the media team.

The team then decided to set him a real challenge. When a bus stopped, they told him to approach the six-foot-two, 230 pounds, mean, tough bus driver and offer him a hug. Lee did this. The bus driver accepted the hug and continued with his task. This left the media team speechless.

Lee was then taken to a home for the disabled. He was not comfortable with this, because he had never hugged people that were terminally ill, severely retarded or quadriplegic. But he believed in his message, and hugged people that he otherwise would never have noticed or approached. There was one particularly disabled man that was drooling on his bib. This man was a real challenge for Lee, but he bent down and hugged the man.

The next moment the man began to squeal, and the other patients clanged items together to express their joy. When Lee turned to the medical staff for an explanation, they were all crying. It was the first time in 23 years that this man had smiled.

 How can you practice Love in your daily life?

It seems possible, or even probable, that we can heal the world by healing the part of ourselves which created the part of the world that needs healing.

Justice always has consequences. The one consequence that we tend to overlook when we demand justice is the effect that any such action will have on ourselves.

Of course, this approach of offering justice with love will not satisfy the public demand that is often based on an eye for an eye. People have been conditioned for thousands of years to demand retribution. However, it is possible to swing the pendulum to rather demand love, and if it takes another thousand years to do this, it will be a job well done.

5 HEARD THE ONE ABOUT THE ELEPHANT AND THE ANT?

Did you know that there is an ant colony that lives on three continents? Seriously. There is a colony of Argentine ants that has spread to Europe and Japan, of course with some help from people. One colony spreads over 6 000 km (3 700 miles) along the Mediterranean coast. The second one extends over 900 km (560 miles) in California in the US. The third colony is in Japan. Researchers discovered that these ant colonies share a very similar type of hydrocarbons in their cuticles, and they are in fact members of the same colony.

Here is the interesting part. Put ants from different colonies together and they become aggressive. Put ants from the same original colony together, and they act like old friends. They are never aggressive towards another, and they never avoid one another. They recognize each other based on the chemical composition of their cuticles.

How many families can associate with this? How many families are spread across the world and feel such strong familial bonds that they will recognize and support their relatives wherever they find them? Draw the circle even closer. How many nuclear families live in the same country and find it difficult to keep contact with each other? It is even more tragic when a family lives in the same town and manages to erect artificial boundaries to keep away from each other. Maybe we can learn from these ants and re-assess our own family bonds.

Do they not contact me because I do not contact them? Do I not contact them because they do not contact me?

 Which relatives have you not contacted for a long time purely because you believe you are right?

When you point a finger to them, see how many fingers point right back to you. It is interesting that whenever you have trouble with various family members, you are the common denominator in all those difficulties. And close physical contact is not the only way to keep family bonds strong. Simply thinking of people with love, wherever they are in the world, is already a step in the right direction.

Another interesting fact about ants is that they understand when we talk to them. Yes, I thought the same when I first heard that. I was told that when you have ants in your house, you can let them leave by talking to them. You use your finger to draw a line where you see the ants, and you simply tell them that it is time for them to leave because they are in danger if they stay. I tried that, and it worked – in two different houses, and with two different groups of ants.

And then there is the interesting fact that elephants are very afraid of bees. At first glance you would think this is probably an urban myth. There is no way a bee can scare an elephant or get through the thick skin of an elephant, right? An elephant skin is about 2.5 cm (1 inch) thick and there is no way that a bee's sting can penetrate that, right? Right. But the elephant's skin is as thin as paper behind the ears, by the eye, on the abdomen, chest and shoulders. And can you imagine how a bee sting could hurt in an elephant's trunk when they have no way to remove that tiny sting once it is nestled in the trunk?

Bees seem to know that, and elephants have discovered this the hard way. Elephants have learnt to stay very far away from bees. An elephant will never eat from a tree that has a bee colony in it – they would not even go near the tree. The elephants can smell bee hives (even empty hives) from a distance and will do anything to avoid the hives.

What probably adds to the fear of the elephants is that when a bee stings, it releases alarm pheromones. When this happens, other bees in the area are attracted and they continue the attack. And getting under water to fool the bees only helps while you are under water. When you surface, the bees will smell the pheromones again and continue with their attack.

Farmers in Kenya are using this fear of bees to control elephants and protect their crops. The farmers had in the past lost many crops through marauding elephants. In recent years, the farmers simply put empty bee-hives at a distance of a few feet apart around their fields. They discovered that the elephants will not even come near enough the fields to confirm that the bee hives are empty.

So, even the mighty elephant has its weak spots and its own fears.

I wish I had known that when I had to deal with corporate elephants and others who walked over me when I was emotionally vulnerable. An old dog is never too old to learn new tricks.

Have you ever used the vulnerabilities of others against them? How did that make you feel?

6 HOLD YOUR HORSES

Have you ever heard the expression 'What you see is what you get'? What if what you see only gets you into trouble, because it is not what you get?

I once read a paragraph that made me sit up and think: "Everything that I see happening around me has a meaning that I have given to it. When I am willing to let go of thinking that I know the real meaning, I notice that it is much different from what I thought it was. Today I realize and understand that the meaning I give to anything has nothing to do with its real purpose. *I do not know the real meaning of what I see.*"

We like to react emotionally and jump to conclusions, often regardless of the facts. Even when we do know the facts, we associate with the facts from our own perspective and do not bother getting the other side of the story, because our own versions are usually right.

 When was the last time you jumped to conclusions, only to be proven wrong?

Here is a Welsh folk tale that shows the danger of acting in haste and not confirming the other side of a story.

Prince Llywelyn of Gwynedd was given a large grey Irish wolfhound as a present from his father-in-law, King John of England. This hound, which he named Gelert, became his favorite, and accompanied him on all his hunting trips. One morning Prince Llywelyn went on a hunting trip to the mountains of Eryri, or Snowdonia in Wales. He called and called, but Gelert was nowhere to be seen. No matter how many times the hunting horn was blown, Gelert was nowhere to be found.

Prince Llywelyn was unhappy about this because Gelert was the fastest and bravest of all the hounds, and they both enjoyed the hunting. But

Prince Llywelyn and his men did not want to wait, and set off from the hunting lodge without Gelert. It was not a good day, and Prince Llywelyn and his men returned earlier than usual.

While the servants stabled the horses, Prince Llywelyn went back to the hunting lodge. He found the door partly open, and the house was dead quiet, which was unusual. An ice-cold hand gripped his heart when he realized that his young son had been left in a cradle upstairs that morning with the servants.

Prince Llywelyn rushed up the stairs and found that everything was overturned and smashed. The maidservants were nowhere to be seen and there was blood everywhere. The cradle was lying on its side, empty. Gelert was lying on the floor, his jaws covered in blood and wagging his tail.

Prince Llywelyn was blind with fury at the betrayal of his favorite hound that had killed the baby boy, and his only thought was of revenge. He drew his sword and violently stabbed Gelert in the heart.

Gelert gave a low moan, but did not move, and then fell sideways, dead.

There was an answering cry from a pile of rags in the corner of the room. Prince Llywelyn looked under the rags and there was his baby boy, safe and sound. Gelert had defended the baby against intruders, and paid with his life.

In memory of his faithful dog, Llywelyn had a grave dug for him, outside his lodge, and erected a carved stone to mark the spot. The village which later grew up nearby was called after this, Beddgelert, the Grave of Gelert.

 If you could turn back the clock, what would you like to undo? Why?

This story is only a few hundred years old.

There is an even older Mongolian version that describes a king who went out hunting with his hawk. One day the king was tired and thirsty, and sat down next to a spring to have a drink.

The king filled his cup with the clear spring water, but before he could drink it, his hawk knocked over the cup with his wings, spilling the water on the ground. The king swore at the bird, and refilled the cup with spring water. Again, the hawk knocked over the cup, and the king cuffed the bird out of the way. The king filled the cup a third time, holding tightly onto it, but the hawk dug his talons into the king's wrist to make him drop it. The king lost his temper, drew his sword and cut off the hawk's head.

When the king picked up the cup again, he looked up and noticed a snake sitting on the rock above the spring, dripping its venom down into the spring water. The hawk had been protecting the king.

These two stories confirm that having a knee-jerk reaction to situations, followed up by false accusations and hasty actions that we regret later, are as old as our memories.

Remember this: *I do not know the real meaning of what I see.*

7 WATCH YOUR THOUGHTS

Are you contributing to crime by reading the newspapers?

Yes, a shocking allegation, but hear me out.

Let me give the background first. There have been at least eighteen victims of knife crime in London over the period of eight months since January 2008. Newspaper reports indicate that the number of people charged with knife crimes have fallen by 50%, and at the same time the number of teenage murders involving knifes have risen dramatically.

A teenager who lives in one of the most dangerous areas in London was quoted as saying "How are the police or the government going to be able to sort this out if we as kids don't know why this sort of stuff's going on?" This child is very wise.

The response of the local government was a website called *London Against Gun and Knife Crime* (http://www.london.gov.uk/gangs/ is no longer available). Obviously, the creators of the website have never heard of the Law of Attraction.

How does this Law of Attraction work? I will give you my understanding of how it works. We think thoughts and these thoughts create waves all around us. The waves resonate with similar waves and then we attract the similar waves to us. The whole process snowballs until our thoughts materialize.

 What do you think you attracted to yourself purely by thinking too much about it?

Let me give you an example. You read the newspaper. There are articles about crime and bad news and negativity all over the pages. You do not think about this and step back and say 'I want love in my life". You read it all and think "I hope I don't ever get mugged.'

Imagine a massive ear listening to your thoughts – an unbiased ear. The ear will not hear the word 'don't' because the ear is unbiased and does not judge – we add the judgment. The ear hears 'hope' and 'mugged'.

Over the next weeks and months, you continue to read the newspapers every day, and for some reason all the articles about muggings and violent crimes catch your eye. Every time you read such an article, you think a similar thought, for example 'More muggings – I wonder who is next.' The massive ear hears 'muggings' and 'next'. Or you think "one of these days someone close to me will get mugged" and the massive ear hears 'someone' and 'me' and 'mugged'.

Then the cousin of the sister of the brother-in-law of a friend's friend gets mugged and you hear about it. Somehow it confirms the thoughts you have had about mugging and you say "I told you so". The next 'logical' thought in your mind is "one of these days I will get mugged". The massive ear still does not judge – like a robot that is there to simply obey commands and to act. The ear hears 'I' and 'get mugged'. And the ear puts you in touch with similar waves around you and your own wave of fear and trepidation and anticipation gets stronger – you just 'know' it will happen to you one day.

Because your thoughts are so full of avoiding being mugged, that is all you think about. You see potential muggers around every corner and cling to your purse or keep ensuring that everything is still in your pocket. And potential muggers pick up on the waves of fear that emanate from you and get closer to you, because you reflect their reality as well.

And then one day you get mugged.

Do you then say 'Oops, time to change my thought processes? Time to raise my thought vibrations and think about unconditional love and peace and things that make me feel good'?

Or do you join the growing chorus of negativity around you and tell everyone in sight of the terrible experience you had, and add momentum to the waves of fear and anxiety around you? And do you, by telling your story and reading more newspapers and watching more TV news to validate your experience, perpetuate the crime around you?

You tell me.

 How much value do you attach to the news? Do you believe all the main news items?

Mother Teresa understood the Law of Attraction. Here is a quote from her: 'I was once asked why I don't participate in anti-war demonstrations. I said that I will never do that, but as soon as you have a pro-peace rally, I'll be there.'

Mother Teresa intuitively understood that what you fill your mind with is what you attract to you.   And where you have an expectation, eventually it will get fulfilled.

How about this explanation for the Law of Attraction: You walk into a restaurant with a friend, order food from the menu, and continue with your conversation.   You expect that your order will be delivered, and guess what, it happens.   And if the order was delivered promptly by a friendly waiter and the food was delicious, you leave a tip to show your gratitude.

Then you walk out of the restaurant, forget all about the Law of Attraction, and get home safely despite having your mind full of thoughts of muggings and what else, and you forget to say 'thank You for bringing me home safely.'

So, we manage to get the less important things, like ordering a meal and paying a tip, right, but then we mess up on the big things, like filling our minds with love and peace and gratitude.   Let's try again and let's this time ensure the massive ear hears only what we want it to hear.   And when the massive ear delivers on what we wanted, let's remember to feel and show gratitude.

 What would you like to attract to yourself?   How can you choose your words so that you are as clear as possible on what you want?

8 HOW TO APPORTION BLAME

Have you ever found yourself in a situation where you knew you were doing a stupid thing, but somehow you could not stop yourself? Then you would also know how it feels to be unable to kick your own backside, and you are too embarrassed to tell anyone else to do it. I will tell you about this because I know I can trust you not to tell anyone else.

My nightmare started with a green car. If I were the Queen, I would have outlawed green cars.

Here is what happened. I owned a green car. I did not use it that often, because it was my second car – I initially bought the car to do someone else a favor, and that is never a good reason to spend money, because such a good deed always comes back to bite you.

When the road tax disc for the car expired, I renewed it on-line – one of the blessings of living in England is easy access to such on-line services. The tax disk arrived in the mail, and I put it in the kitchen with other stuff that I was going to deal with eventually – no rush, because I was not using the car every day.

Then one day I came home, only to find that some road workers had broken into the car during the day and moved it while I was away. Their excuse? They had to dig up the road – no forward notice of any kind to the neighborhood – and the car was in the way. The tax disc was not up to date, and although they had the facilities to check, they preferred to assume that the car was abandoned. And – hear this – they did not damage the car when they broke into it, so what exactly was I complaining about?

Of course, this kind of behavior is just not on for me, and I went to the police but nothing came of it. The reason was that in England the law says something like if I was at home I would have moved the car for the road workers to do their job, and therefore their breaking into the car without my knowledge or permission was not illegal. Yes, I also thought that England was a civilized country where crime is not tolerated.

Of course, the next day I used the car to go to work, so that the road workers would not have another opportunity to practice their part-time profession. I was not happy with this, because somehow, I knew the car and everything that was associated with it was bad news.

On the way home, I ran out of petrol – for the first time ever in my life. The bloody car did it again! Of course, I could not leave the car on a yellow line – trust a green car to die on a yellow line – and had to pay an arm and a leg to have the car towed home. I left the stupid car at home to suffer, and went away for a weekend with friends.

When I returned, she was there, waiting for me with an empty tank. Somehow, I know that car was female. I went to the petrol station, bought a petrol can and filled it with petrol – after first showering myself in petrol because I did not realize the force of the petrol stream into the empty can would result in a spray of petrol over my hair, face and clothes. Bloody green car!

I went home, filled the tank with petrol and started the car – and quickly found a buyer for the car. Our parting was not amicable.

 Can you recall the last time you did one stupid thing after another and could not stop yourself, even if you knew you were wrong?

OK, now you can stop laughing. And you can criticize me for getting emotional about such a petty thing, once you can convince me that nothing like this has ever happened to you.

Why was I traumatized by a green car? Because I focused on the effects rather than on the cause. And I am supposed at this point in my journey to know better. Just shows you that we never stop learning.

Of course, if I had put the updated tax disk in the car, the road workers might have listened to my neighbors who told them that I owned the car. This might not have deterred them, but the tax disk was still my responsibility and I did not do it.

It was also my responsibility to ensure that there was enough petrol in the car before using it. And the worst part is that instead of having the car towed in, I could have walked the short distance to the petrol station and saved myself about 90% of the money I spent on getting the car towed back home. At the time, I was so fed up that I did not think straight.

Of course, when we accept that we create all our experiences - no matter how good or bad they are - our entire view of the world changes. Instead of fighting for our place in the world, we create as much or as little space for ourselves in the world as we want, and it becomes so much easier to get what we want.

My story relates to a car, but we tend to do the same with just about everything else in our lives. Think of the people that treat you badly in a relationship or a friendship – but you allow them to treat you in that manner because unconsciously you have to learn much from them about yourself. This is the case with relationships everywhere – even casual incidents with people that you do not know. And the opposite is true as well – people treat you well when unconsciously you expect them to treat you well.

 What is the worst experience you have ever created for yourself? And the best?

I once was waiting for a train when a young man approached me. The first thing I noticed was the tattoo that covered his entire head, and things that to me looked like ball-bearings that were implanted under his scalp, not to mention all the other pieces of metal sticking out of him that must have caused him tremendous discomfort.

My first instinct was to turn away and look for the safety of other people. But then I saw his eyes and realized he was a funny-looking kid who was stressed and lost. He asked me about a particular train, and I immediately realized that he was on the wrong platform, because the names of two stations were very similar. I told him where to go to catch his train, and he was so grateful when he ran up the stairs.

 When was the last time you were deceived by the appearance of a person and misjudged them?

The only thing he 'did to me' was remind me that looks may be deceiving and that we choose how we respond to people. When we are at cause (we recognize our own creation), we get a perspective that is completely different from when we are at effect (we assume we are victims of circumstances).

Another area of our lives that we plan very well and then blame elsewhere is our physical health. Think about dis-ease. Every single dis-ease that we experience is our own creation. Dis-ease is an expression of the part of our soul or subconscious that we need or want to focus on in our quest to learn everything about ourselves that we planned for this existence.

In the meantime, I have realized that green cars, and especially troublesome green cars, are in fact a blessing. That particular car had to teach me the difference between taking responsibility for my creation and blaming everyone in sight for what I created. Why am I talking about the car as if it is a person? Simply because the car is energy, just like I am energy. Who says it is not alive? Just joking – or am I?

9 CHANGING FIRST AND SECOND IMPRESSIONS

I am fascinated by how the mind and brain works and how our thought processes are shaped.

How do we grow new habits? How do we change our thought processes?

I read an analogy the other day that made a lot of sense to me.

The author compared our minds to a piece of paper that is folded. Try this: fold a piece of paper. Then fold it again. Put the piece of paper down. When you pick it up, the easiest fold to reach is the most recent one.

Our thoughts are the same. Whenever we have a new thought, our minds return to the most recent thought. This is an incredibly powerful piece of information.

Here is another fact. Our minds and bodies by default tune to positive thoughts. One positive thought will counter-act several negative thoughts.

What does all this mean?

It means we can control our thoughts. When we do that, we control both the energy waves that emanate from us, and the energy that returns to us.

This is such a simple, yet powerful tool.

Imagine a new colleague joins the team at work. I see this person for the first time and notice her lovely eyes. That is the first fold in the paper. Then this person does not introduce herself to me, and her first words are criticism against her predecessor for not clearing the desk drawers before she arrived. My impression of a very rude woman is the second and most recent fold in the paper.

The newcomer sits at a desk five steps from my own desk. I still do not know her name. I have forgotten about her lovely eyes. I now think of her as 'that rude woman at the next desk'. This thought then becomes the most recent fold in the paper.

But is she really rude? Could it be that she is insecure, and that the new desk represents a temporary position that she does not really want to have anyway, and that she was in fact voicing her frustration? Was that the reason why she raised her voice and neglected to introduce herself? Could it be only my perception that she is rude?

When someone then enters the office, and ask where Lynne's desk is, I have no idea who Lynne is. If someone then points at the desk of the new lady, my first thought is 'they mean the rude lady' because that was the most recent thought about her in my mind.

I do not think 'they mean the new lady with the beautiful eyes', because that original thought has been covered with more recent thoughts. My mind habitually returns to the most recent thought on the topic.

Then I am away from work for a few days. When I return, the lady walks into the office, approaches my desk, holds out her hand and says 'Hi. We have not been introduced yet. My name is Lynne'". She smiles and I think 'she has lovely eyes'. That becomes the most recent thought about her in my mind.

I can still go back to the thought of 'the rude new lady', but suddenly it is not that easy. My new thought is about 'Lynne with the lovely eyes', and this thought feels much better.

Every time I now attempt to think about 'the rude lady' I feel an unpleasant physical reaction in my body. However, when I think of Lynne with the lovely eyes, I have a different, far more pleasant physical sensation.

We go through this process every day without even being conscious of our thoughts.

 Have you over the past months changed your mind about a person or situation? How did the change start? What made you change your mind?

The power of this is that when we become conscious of this process, we can immediately identify a thought that does not resonate with our selves. We can then examine that thought, and replace it with another thought that does resonate with our selves.

Of course, with the awareness of the power of our thoughts comes awareness of our selves.

We have all at some stage been involved in an argument where we said things in the heat of the moment and really felt good about winning the argument by being the most hurtful party, only to cringe the next day when we remember what we had said.

Have you ever been involved in some activities with people that at the time felt very good (often under the influence of alcohol or with youthful exuberance), like mercilessly teasing or even bullying other people? And the next day you are so embarrassed about your behavior that you don't even want to associate with your friends, because they remind you of your moments of weakness.

When we become aware of how positive thoughts resonate with us while negative thoughts trigger feelings of discomfort, it becomes easier to immediately replace negative thoughts with positive thoughts.

 Which thoughts make you feel uncomfortable? How would you like to change those thoughts?

Over time it becomes easier to ensure the most recent thought is one that resonates with us and reflects our true loving selves.

While we are in the habit of resonating negative thoughts without an awareness of the impact on our bodies, we feel that replacing those thoughts with positive thoughts is a bit of a strain. However, over a period, thinking the positive thoughts becomes a habit, and we then try to avoid the negative thoughts.

This is like learning to play the piano. When you focus on the white keys, you manage to play reasonably well. However, when you really make an effort to use the black keys as well, suddenly there is a different, richer, more complete sound that you can control at will. When you reach this level of mastery, playing on the white keys only sounds hollow.

It is possible for us to master our thoughts. The negative thoughts will leave kicking and screaming, but they will leave, if that is what we want for ourselves.

10 CLOSING THE CHAPTER ON BULLIES

Throughout my life, I have had to deal with bullies. Some of my first memories are of my mother mistreating me physically and emotionally. I encountered numerous bullies as colleagues, and too many of them used me for target practice. I also married a man who nearly destroyed me emotionally, and I had other relationships and friendships that did nothing for my self-esteem.

The treatment I had from my mother led me to much introspection. I just could not understand why she disliked me so much. It took me years to realize that her role in my life was to teach me to understand my own value. I had to realize that my self-worth does not come from the people in my life, but from the way I look at myself. Do I recognize my own worth? Or do I wait for others to convince me that God knew what he was doing when he created me?

My mother has since passed on, and with my understanding of her behavior came peace. We now have a good relationship and I honor her as one of the greatest teachers of my life.

 Which person had the biggest influence on your life because they mistreated you?

I recently had a fascinating experience. I was on an overnight flight from Johannesburg to Istanbul. When I checked in I asked for an aisle seat because I like to stretch my legs without disturbing other passengers. I was told that there were no aisle seats available.

Early in the flight, I noticed a vacant aisle seat three rows back from where I was sitting. There was a man sitting in the window seat. I asked a stewardess whether I could move to the aisle seat, and she said it was OK.

There were some newspapers and overnight blankets on the seat. The man in the window seat made no effort to remove these items and just looked at me picking up the newspapers and blankets and putting them under the seat. He was wide awake while I sat down and fastened my seatbelt.

I settled down and fell asleep.

About three hours later the man woke me up because he wanted to go to the toilet. I got up to let him pass. He stood in the aisle and told me that I had stepped on his newspapers which he had paid for (to me they looked just like the newspapers that the staff handed out after take-off. They were Turkish newspapers and the man spoke with an accent that gave away the fact that English was not his first language.) He demanded in a loud voice that I pick up the newspapers and put them where I found them. He then pranced away to the toilet.

My first concern was for the rest of the passengers. Nobody wants a fuss at 2.30am in a confined space. I picked up the newspapers and put them on the man's seat. I also had the distinct impression that this man had been badly hurt by someone and that he was very angry at life in general.

When he returned from the toilet, he told me that I had taken his blanket that was also on the seat and demanded in a very loud voice that I move back to my original seat. I picked up one of the two sealed blankets from under the seat and handed the blanket to the man, still saying nothing.

The man demanded again that I move back to my original seat. I calmly asked him how many seats he had paid for, and this resulted in another tirade. I then told him that I had permission to use the seat.

He went to sit down, and slammed the newspapers onto my seat. I sat down, held the newspapers out to him and politely asked whether he wanted the newspapers on his lap or on the floor. He grabbed the newspapers and bundled them into the seat pocket in front of me. He then told me that I was 'unmannered' – I think he meant disobedient. I did not respond to any of this and simply settled down to sleep again. I fell asleep immediately.

 How did you respond the last time you dealt with a bully?

When we were served breakfast the next morning, the man had two bread rolls and I had none. I offered him my butter, but he only mumbled and did not even look up.

At this point the cabin lights were on, and I could get a better view of the man. He was one of those men who are balding and refusing to accept the fact. One of the first things he did was to meticulously comb his remaining hair to cover his bald spot. I also noticed that he looked slightly sleazy, even though his suit was obviously expensive. I had a feeling that he was quite insecure, and that my lack of response to his bullying probably added to his insecurity. I felt sorry for him.

As we left the plane, I noticed him fawning over a young woman who looked slightly frightened. I had the impression that they were colleagues, and I realized that his middle-of-the-night tirade was probably also aimed at proving some point to her, because she was sitting opposite the aisle in the same row and had heard everything.

Two days after the incident I still caught myself thinking about the incident. I was wondering why I was giving a complete stranger so much head space.

Then I realized that my memories were focused on my own inner experience and not on the man. I remembered how I felt during the entire incident. It was as if I was outside of my body, looking on to the situation. I felt complete peace and tranquility while this man was ranting – as if it was happening to someone else.

Most of what I recalled from the incident focused on the fact that I did not respond to the man's insults and attitude. I felt no emotion. I felt no desire to attack him, or even to defend myself. I felt like a spectator standing on a river bank, watching a branch swirling and desperately trying to latch onto anything that would get it out of the turmoil of the water.

I realized that this incident underlined a closing chapter in my own life. I had dealt with all the bullies in my life and moved on. I had thanked them all for teaching me very valuable lessons about myself. I thanked them with pure gratitude and no condescension.

 What kind of behaviour from others have you learnt to manage by becoming emotionally detached?

I felt that this man was some sort of final test for me. He did his best to needle me with very unreasonable behavior, and I barely noticed it. I did not feel threatened at all. I did not feel hurt. I felt his own deep hurt and my heart went out to him. During the entire incident and afterwards I found myself in a place where there is only peace, tranquility and compassion.

When I discovered all this, I felt a deep gratitude and Love. I realized that I had already closed the book on the life theme of being bullied and discovering my self-worth.

I am ready to move on and use this experience to help others achieve the same inner peace.

11 THE SPIRITUAL PURPOSE OF TELLING LIES

Whoa, you say. How can lying ever serve a purpose when you are a spiritual person? Surely it is better for all involved to always tell the truth?

Let me give you an example of two people who told lies for different reasons. I am not judging them or saying I have never told a lie. I am simply recognizing a truth here that I have not been aware of, namely that there are times when lies serve a spiritual purpose.

 Have you ever felt justified in telling a lie? Who did you protect? What was the result?

Two girls (Annie and Laura) were best friends in school. After school, they both married young and stayed in touch, but the longer they both were married, the more their emotional closeness became watered down. They were both aware of it, but never discussed it.

Then one day Annie deliberately told Laura a few lies. Of course, Laura was shocked and hurt, and did not understand why Annie went out of her way to destroy their friendship.

Annie and Laura went their separate ways and lost contact for fifteen years. Then a string of co-incidences resulted in their paths crossing again. It so happened that Laura contacted Annie the day after Annie's ex-husband had died.

It was like finding a comfortable cardigan again that had been mislaid for many years. In a few sentences, Annie explained that she had to break off contact with Laura and all her loved ones, including her family, in a misguided attempt to please her husband and salvage her marriage. By the time she realized that her marriage was doomed anyway, she no longer had the contact details of people that would have been able and willing to support her.

Laura then understood that at the time she was also not ready to provide Annie with the support she needed.

All these years Annie's lies and the loss of their friendship had bothered Laura, and Laura admitted blaming Annie for it. Laura had no idea that them being separated was part of both their life paths, and that this was part of the Bigger Plan.

 Have you ever lost contact with a person because of lies? How did you deal with it?

Laura also had a relative, Andrew, who enjoyed telling deliberate lies. Andrew had been dishonest in his marriage and living an illusion by fooling and lying to and cheating family and friends for many years.

As the saying goes, you can fool some of the people some of the time, but you cannot fool all the people all the time.

Andrew's lies had reached a point of desperation, where he was resorting to emotionally blackmailing his children and the small group of family member and friends that still have contact with him.

Of course, the easiest way is to judge Andrew and to get irritated about him not growing up and facing reality.

But what if all his lies, as with Annie, served a purpose for him as well? What if those lies are part of their life paths, which is different from ours? What if everyone that get fed up with their dishonesty, play a significant role in helping them to learn valuable lessons in their lives? Then surely, we should each simply hold up our versions of the truth each time it differs from their version of the truth, and in that way, help them to learn their lesson so that they can move on to a smoother path?

I have realized that lies are simply a truth that is not mine, and it is not for me to judge the actions and motives of another person when they live a different truth.

 How do you deal with a person who often tells lies? Do you confront them about it or do you ignore them? What is best for you?

Lies are a part of the life path of each of us. If you disagree, think of the last time you lied or bent the truth to achieve a purpose. We can judge others for lying to us, or we can take responsibility for every time we present our own truth, and understand that we determine our own life paths.

God loves us all, and that is not a lie.

12 INNER CONFLICT AND OUTER TENSION

Life is stressful. Many people try to relieve their stress by taking some form of chemical crutch like a sleeping pill, alcohol or a cigarette. None of these helps to relieve stress. They simply suppress the symptoms of stress.

 What do you use for stress relief? Why?

Stress is not caused by life events such as moving house or getting divorced or changing jobs. All these and many other events are external symptoms of an inner division which is expressed as physical stress.

The way people deal with stressful events also differs drastically from one person to the next. For example, one person gets raped and carries that burden for the rest of her life. She knows of no other way to define herself. Another person gets raped and experiences a turning point in her life where she becomes a motivational speaker or changes to a highly successful career that she would otherwise never have considered.

Stress is nothing other than an inner division or inner tension. This tension is determined by how the person perceives the situation. What is healthy stress for one person is unhealthy stress for another person. Healthy stress results in inner growth towards maturity. Unhealthy stress results in stagnation, and emotional and physical pain.

 What stress are you experiencing at the moment? Is it healthy or unhealthy stress?

A life event can be stressful for one person, but a relief for another person. One person dreads moving house, while another person looks forward to a change in environment.

What happens when you ignore or suppress the symptoms of stress? Your body finds more and more different ways to express the tension. If you believe that chemicals and drugs resolve stress, you add more chemicals to your cocktail and your body protests more and more. It becomes a vicious circle.

How can you avoid the consequences of ignored stress?

First acknowledge the symptoms of your stress and then look for the cause. Sometimes this is easy, and at other times it is a challenge to first overcome the fear of what you may find when you do some introspection.

 What is the cause of your stress? Why do you have inner tension? How does your body express the stress?

When you take that step, and explore the reason for your inner tension, you will always find an inner conflict. That conflict has two sides – counter-arguments if you wish. Your stress increases as the arguments for either side becomes stronger. This is what you express in your physical body. The physical stress breaks the moment you realize that both your inner arguments are yours and correct, and you can choose to use those arguments depending on the situation you experience and your judgment. At that moment relief floods your body and you can relax.

Sounds like it is worth entering a meditative state when you are stressed out, so that you can get to the source of the stress faster and resolve it.

13 EVER-LASTING PEACE? I THINK NOT

What would an Israeli ex-soldier, a Northern Irish child of peace fighters, an Arab with terrorist siblings and a product of South African apartheid have in common?

Would you expect all these people to demand peace and denounce war? Probably.

However, here is a completely different take.

Think back to the last time when you had a moment of complete peace. Can you remember what you experienced? Was it stillness, or bliss? Can you remember the calmness? Now imagine that your moment of peace continues for a long time – like five years with no interruption. Wouldn't that be nice?

I thought not.

I made a list of the drawbacks of such a long spell of peace. My list included a lack of personal growth. What do we learn from the good times?

 If you had to make a list of the negative consequences of peace in your life, what would they be?

Of course, there would be no challenge, because everyone will agree that this peace is wonderful, and there is no challenge in similarity.

Just the thought of all this makes me feel bored already. I do not particularly enjoy fighting or arguing, but I cannot imagine that a long period of being unchallenged by anything will be anything less than boring. It is great to feel placid and quiet, but as the saying goes, too much of a good thing is no longer good.

Have you ever had a real fight on your hands and then experienced peace afterwards? I can remember many instances where I achieved that peace, and enjoyed all of it. If I did not first experience the conflict, I would probably not have appreciated the peace.

 What part of your life are you at peace about? What price did you pay for that peace?

I enjoy having my attention and energy focused on some objective. There are times when I simply focus on clearing my mind so that I can receive creative thoughts and energy. What if I receive all that energy and I am so at peace with myself and the world that I just allow the energy to flow away through my fingers? Possibly once, maybe twice, and after that I will get itchy. That is my nature.

I feel that everlasting peace will be a denial of life. We do not live in a world where there is always peace. Even when we live in a peaceful country, we always experience some inner turmoil based on love, work or social relationships. If no other people are involved, we still have some sort of inner turmoil. Life is about not having peace and always striving towards peace.

Of course, there is another side to every situation – like a coin which always has two sides.

 Think back to a situation that you can describe as your own war. Was it a war where you were a soldier? Or was it an argument, or a conflict situation that you did not enjoy at all? Was it inner turmoil where you had to make peace with some changes in your life?

Here is the interesting question: what did you gain from the situation?

One of the main things I have gained from war – even if it is just conflict with another person, is an appreciation of diversity. We are not the same. There are a few billion different people on this planet. Every one of us has something to contribute to humanity.

I have experienced inner conflict situations where I assumed that various people were the enemy. I have on many occasions been surprised to discover empathy and compassion in others, and this has taught me humility.

Conflict situations have allowed me to experience gratitude for what I have and for what I have gained from the conflict. I have learnt to look for the upside of every conflict situation and for the downside of every situation that was based on an infatuation with a person or circumstances. As a result, my life has become far more balanced. I have learnt to control and manage my emotions, rather than allow strong emotions to manage me.

What wisdom have you gained from your past conflict?

Have you noticed that with any conflict you get to a point where you have clarity of vision? You move above and beyond the conflict and as a result you see the so-called bigger picture. Suddenly you realize how petty and insignificant your conflict is, and you experience the relief that goes with peace.

Have you ever had conflict with a love partner, and as a result experienced even deeper love based on increased understanding? Now there is a moment of peace that I would not exchange for anything.

Looking back at my life, conflict has allowed me to cut ties with people and move on. Often, we hold on to people to the detriment of everyone involved. Conflict allows us to let go and grow into greater things. Sadly, we hardly ever stop to thank our opponents for allowing us to leave them behind.

 Have you had to leave people behind in your life? Did you ever stop to thank them for what they have taught you about yourself and life?

Conflict also often forces us to change direction. Remember that vicious boss who eventually made you resign in desperation? Remember how you got a far better job which allowed you to grow and learn more about yourself? Imagine still being stuck in that going-nowhere-fast relationship and not meeting the next person who was ready for the new you.

War and peace do not only happen between countries. We have war and peace inside of ourselves and around us daily.

Next time you wish for peace, remember that peace will not last. Neither will war. We need peace as much as we need conflict. That is the purpose of our existence here.

Of course, needing conflict does not mean needing to kill other people. Just step back and see what you can learn from yourself about the conflict. Then thank your opponent for the lesson and move on.

14 WHAT DO PEOPLE SAY ABOUT YOU?

Do you ever listen to what people say about you? Do you take other people's opinions about you seriously?

This is my personal guideline for what people say about me: If someone tells you that you are a horse, laugh it off - they are obviously having a bad day and it has nothing to do with you. If a second person tells you that you are a horse, look in the mirror - they may have a point. If a third person tells you that you are a horse, enter the Grand National, because they are telling the truth.

Our auras, what we say and how we behave reflect our inner state. People respond to the energy they pick up from us, and they act as mirrors for us. We need to be aware of what other people see in the mirror.

 What have people said about you? Did you act on it or laugh it off?

For example, a person feels inferior and unloved and expresses himself with verbal attacks on other people to prove at all costs that he is right. He is advised to change his approach and say 'Have you considered this aspect?' rather than say 'You are so stupid - I know better and you must listen to me'.

He does not hear the advice and continues with his behavior. Then someone else says 'Try saying: There are two sides to this. Here is one side and here is the other side. What do you think?' rather than 'How can you talk such drivel? Let me tell you the truth, and listen carefully, because I am the master.'

However, the ego is still in the way, until one day when someone says 'I cannot hear a word of what you are saying, because I am overwhelmed by how you are talking!' Sadly, a really good message goes completely unnoticed, because the messenger gets in the way of the message. The result is a person who feels even lonelier and more unloved.

Sometimes we also hide a talent because of the same blind spot. For example, a person is always doodling and making little drawings. Somebody says 'That is beautiful - why don't you do it more often?' and the response is 'No, this is nothing' and the drawings are hidden away.

Then a friend enters some of the drawings into a competition, and the unwilling artist wins - but runs away from the publicity and still says 'it is nothing'.

Other friends notice this talent and ask for drawings. The artist feels comfortable with the requests, and slowly, slowly starts to trust the creative flow. He builds up confidence to the point where he not only responds to requests, but also experiments with new techniques. Then one day he realizes that he can trust his talent, and the resulting works of art are incredibly beautiful because they come from a sacred space.

 Think of the things people have told you that you can do. Have you at least tried? Why?

You cannot reject the reflection in your mirror forever.

15 HOLD YOUR OWN MEMORIES

Who is in charge of your memories?

I was clearing out some photographs and had to decide whether to keep or delete photographs of people who are no longer part of my life. I decided to keep the photographs because each one of those people made me the person I am today, and I want to take my gratitude for them into the future. I have no desire to destroy them or their images. And this is not emotional baggage either. If I lose the photographs because of my own doing, I will not be devastated.

This reminded me of my first serious adult relationship – a sweet one that was not meant to last. Even at the time I knew that I was out of my depth and I think that contributed to me feeling flattered about the attention I was receiving at the time. When the relationship fizzled out, I felt gratitude and relief and moved on – and kept the photographs and mementos.

Then I had another relationship where my new partner insisted on destroying all those innocent love letters and photographs. At the time, I thought I should feel flattered because of his jealousy and possessiveness, but I just felt bewildered and a sense of loss.

That sense of loss has remained with me until this day. It is not a matter of getting closure or letting go of the previous relationship – that was never relevant.

 Do you have sweet memories without mementos?

Not all memories of a past relationship are 'bad' – or 'good' for that matter. Those memories are part of a path of self-discovery and very personal.

When you hand your memories to another person, no matter what your motivation is, it is in fact the beginning of the end for the new relationship. This is the point where you hand over control of your destiny to your new partner, and where you put a part of yourself on hold. That part of yourself does not go away – it waits until you are ready to deal with it.

I spent the rest of the weekend recalling my rose-colored version of that first relationship – and maybe it was good that there were no photographs or love letters to remind me of the reality – who knows?

 Do you have memories where you would rather hold on to your version than the truth? What have you learnt from that experience?

I only realized recently what I was meant to learn from an incident that happened a lifetime ago – because I am now ready to learn and move on.

16 PLEASE MAKE ME HAPPY

I sometimes get requests from people to help them move to the UK, because they are so unhappy where there are, for various reasons. For example, a man does not like his job in Jordan and sends his CV to me so that I can find him a job in England. Or a woman does not like the cultural constraints on her behavior and actions in Egypt and wants me to help her find an English boyfriend. Or a man in South Africa hears how happy his friends are in England, and decides to move after them and share their happiness.

The one thing that these people have in common is that they want other people to make them happy. They do not know yet that happiness comes from inside, and not from other people.

To put it another way, they feel trapped in their situation and want to escape at all costs to the land of milk and honey, wherever and whoever that is.

Guess what? These are the immigrants who find fault with everything in their adopted country. They cannot find what they came looking for, and go back to their homeland, even more disillusioned than when they arrived in their adopted country.

 Have you ever expected another person to make you happy? Did they meet your expectations?

This happens when someone does not understand one of the basic laws of nature, namely that for every action there is an equal and opposite reaction. They live in a bubble of unhappiness and they do not even notice the positive aspects of their situation.

Every situation, no matter how 'bad' it is, has two sides. And we have two options in terms of how to deal with the situation. We can focus entirely on the downside, and find lots of evidence that we are right. Or we can deliberately search for the upside of the situation – because it is there if we care to look for it.

For example, to escape from an unpleasant job my friend has developed a hobby that he can make money from. That will combine his passion with his economic need. He can practice that hobby in Jordan or in England.

The lady could find an English boyfriend and be at his beck and call, so that she can survive in England. How does that differ from being at the beck and call of a man in her own country based on her own culture? She already has many means of coping with her current situation but does not recognize them, because she is looking for a solution from someone else.

And the South Africans who want to come to England in search of happiness? Until they have resolved their emotional issues about their own country, they will not be happy anywhere else in the world.

 What is making you unhappy right now? How can you change the situation without waiting for someone else to do it for you?

If you are unhappy where you are right now, look for the exact opposite of what causes your unhappiness. When you find it, a chemical reaction will take place in your body, and you will change permanently – for the better.

17 NEWSFLASH: UPS AND DOWNS HAPPEN

Are you living your life according to spiritual principles? Is your life perfect because of that?

There are loads of books and gurus out there selling to you the secret to eternal happiness and a life of riches. Of course, if you are in the sad majority (i.e. 99.9% of people on this planet) who experience downs as well as ups, the reason is that you have not followed the rules to achieve constant and amazing success, and that means you failed.

Can we stop there for a moment?

Can you name just one person who lives a life of say 80 years and NEVER experience any setback or disappointment or disillusionment?

Come on, think harder – there must be someone.

Or is life meant to be a balance between joy and sadness, success and disappointment, health and illness, etc. etc.?

 Where have you noticed balance in your life? Where do you not have enough balance?

Why do these gurus create the impression that life is always a bunch of roses, and that when you are scratched by a thorn, it is your fault?

The more I see and experience of life, the more I realize that there is a perfect rhythm of ups and downs in our lives.

So how do we deal with the downs? How about changing the words we use? When we experience ups, the implication is that there we will go down, and the other way round.

I would rather prefer to talk about challenges and gratitude. When I use those words, my life does not necessarily become flawless – if it does, I will check my pulse, because I may be dead and still walking around.

Which negative aspect of your life do you need to own?
What positive spin-off have you never recognized?

When I talk about challenges and gratitude, the emotional see-saw disappears and my path becomes much more balanced. When I then hit a challenge, I do much soul-searching, because I know already that my destination is gratitude. And when I experience gratitude, I know that my next challenge will be bigger, but so will be the opening of my heart in gratitude.

I like to think of that as the pulse of the Universe. It is also called life.

18 THE MOMENT OF FORGIVENESS

We like to think that celebrities live a perfect life, because they are rich and famous. Take for example Angelina Jolie – famous, rich, married to a rich and famous man. What could possibly bother her that she cannot simply buy a solution for?

How about a rift with her father that lasted for ten years? No amount of shopping can take away such hurt.

 Do you have a rift that is still bothering you with someone? What are you gaining from doing nothing about it?

In 2002 Angelina Jolie and her father Jon Voight had a serious argument. As a result, they were publicly estranged until recently. The change in the situation came after what Jon Voight described as an "emotional epiphany" that altered his attitude in a moment.

In an interview, he described a moment when 'everything shifted' and thus the way was opened for him to be re-united with his daughter. He described his gratitude about what happened and said that when he is with his grand-children his daughter 'sees another energy in [him] which takes over'.

There is a fascinating quantum physical process behind what has happened with Jon Voight. And yes, he may say that the solution came in a moment, but that moment in fact took nearly ten years. And at the same time the ten years took only a moment.

This process is all based on two conflicting sides fighting against each other, and finally the two sides become one. This process can go on for years, or it can be resolved in days. The more intense the experience, the greater the moment of wisdom and gratitude is.

Because we were not in his life and in the moment when the conflict started, we will never know the full truth. After all, the truth that is reported in the press is the newsworthy version of what is mostly gossip.

However, in this instance, Jon Voight probably experienced very strong conflicting emotions about his daughter – where he did not want to lose her love and affection, but at the same time he did not want to accept her judgment and rejection.

Such a conflict situation becomes evident when you say, for example, 'part of me wants . . . while another part of me wants . . .'

 How would you describe the opposing parts of your inner conflict? Which part of you is not acceptable? Which part of you is acceptable?

Those two opposing parts struggle against each other until the inner conflict is resolved. In that moment when the resolution happens, you experience a moment of intense gratitude where a quantum of light is formed in every cell of your body, and you get a glimpse of the Universe. Jon Voight came close to it when he described the moment as 'an emotional epiphany'.

In the moment when this change happens, your entire body vibration increases by a notch, and the change in your energy vibration is permanent. That is why his daughter could remark that she sees 'another energy' in him which takes over when he is with his grand-children.

Is it really necessary to carry such a grudge for ten years? Of course not! When you understand the quantum physical process, it is possible to shorten the process to days or even to hours if you are willing to work on it. The longer you carry such a grudge and conflict with you, the more damage you do to your physical and emotional body.

And once you have experienced the success of the process and the means of resolving the conflict, you will understand why we go through these processes and experiences during our lives. You may not necessarily look forward to the next conflict, but you will know the signs and what to expect, and it will be easier to resolve the conflict and move on.

19 WHAT TO DO WITH OLD PHOTOGRAPHS AND MEMORIES

I was working through loads of photographs for a project that requires illustrations.

These photographs took me back to good times, hard times, happy times, times I would rather forget.

There are beautiful moments that I want to relive. I can see the energy and the Love of my grandchildren, and the wisdom in a photo of my dad in his last days.

I can smell some of the scenes again, and hear the noises related to other photos. This made me realize that my photographs are not just visual mementos, but my life history captured.

In some photographs, I can see the people and how they feel about me and about being captured in my memories. Most of these are joyful moments that we all wanted to be reminded off in later years.

However, in other photographs I have images of people and moments that were joyful and loving at the time, and that turned out to be illusions – some of them false illusions with actors that do not have one bone of integrity between all of them.

 Do you keep photographs of people that you no longer want in your life? How do you feel about it?

This is where I asked myself: Do I delete these photographs that leave me wanting to cry because of lost dreams? Or do I keep them and every so often remind myself of what I have learnt from and moved on from?

I realized that if I can still look at these offending photographs and feel any emotion, the work is not done yet. I need to keep them until I get to a point where it does not matter whether I keep or delete them. As long as I see the photographs as representing anything that I don't want or like, the memories are still apart from me. I have not yet got to the point where I can say it does not matter, and mean what I say.

Many years ago, I was in a relationship where I allowed the man to destroy some memories of a previous relationship. I regret that experience to this day because I allowed him to destroy something precious to me, to soothe his own demons. That is another reason why I will press the delete button on these photographs when I am good and ready.

In the meantime, I will park those photographs in a place where I will only notice them if I go and look for them. Out of sight, out of mind, but not out of heart. There will come a day when those memories will be present in every cell of my body, and then I will deal with them.

20 PROMISES AND DELIVERIES

I tend to see myself as not very tactful. As a result, people always know where they stand with me.

However, when I do clairvoyant readings, I am fully aware of the words I use, or rather of the words that are given to me. I am always focused on giving a very clear message to my clients, and on being honest, but at the same time on having empathy for them.

So maybe I am more tactful than I give myself credit for.

The problem is that I tend to expect other people to do the same – to say what they do and do what they say. And as life goes, this does not always happen.

Recently a person who does Chinese face reading told me that an area of my face shows a strong 'bull-shit detector', in other words, don't lie to me or create a picture that is anything but real and honest, because you will not get away with it.

Sadly, this detector had failed me over time. I had expectations of some people and I did everything from my side to help them meet my expectations of them. I was quite sure that I had communicated my expectations in many ways, but apparently, I had not.

 Have people failed you because you did not communicate your expectations clearly?

Recently I had one shock after another, and I realized that after years of knowing these people, I do not know them at all. I felt quite angry, betrayed and disappointed. I contacted them and told them how I felt, but they had nothing to say, and I know that expecting an apology would again be expecting too much. I now need to put this behind me and move on.

What went wrong? I can write an entire page condemning the people involved and pointing a finger, but they will have no idea that I am doing this because they are on the other side of the world, and I will just be in a hell that I created all by myself.

Alternatively, I can look at the three fingers that point back to me while I point my finger at them. Those three fingers tell their own story.

The first finger tells me something I have known for years, namely that you NEVER help another person because you feel pity for the person. When you do that, you take on a burden that another person should carry, and you exhaust your own resources. When you have no resources left, you cannot help yourself and you cannot help those people around you that can benefit from help that comes from objectivity rather than from emotional bias.

 Have you ever helped a person and felt you have lost something precious? What did you learn from it?

There is also the matter of fair exchange. If you help someone and you do not get anything in exchange, nobody is satisfied and it is easy to have negative feelings about what you did. This may sound harsh, but some people will take your help and thank you and make a huge success and help others because of what your actions taught them, while others will always come back for more until you are exhausted, and then they will move on to someone else and suck them dry.

When you expect something in exchange from the person that you help and make that clear, the person knows that your help is a conscious act and they are aware of their own obligation. They can then choose to either honor their obligation or not accept your help, and both people know where they stand. I assumed fair exchange from one person that firmly believes in sucking others dry, and from another person that I thought had the same values that I have, because I did not spell out the rules right from the beginning.

The second finger tells me that in both instances I failed to set expectations clearly. I did communicate my expectations at the beginning of both situations, and I assumed that years of 'bad' habits and 'wrong' ideas will be wiped out in one conversation with me. I was the one that added the judgment, because I applied my view of the world to the person. In their own minds, they are sure that they did the right things for the right reasons.

It is possible to help people change their beliefs and values, but the motivation must come from them and not from me. These changes can be accelerated with various techniques, but it cannot just be done by having one normal conversation. I was dealing with two separate worlds that will hardly ever come together, and I assumed that allowing a person into my view of the world will take away or 'fix' the other person's view of the world. I came down into my own reality very hard. I live my illusion and nobody else's, and I cannot undo the world of another person. That is not what I am here for.

 Have you ever had misunderstandings and judged too harshly?

The third lesson was that once you have said what you do, you must always do what you say and not fear the consequences. I made life very difficult for myself by tolerating and thinking I was being generous, charitable, and helpful. The other people took from me without thinking twice simply because I was giving, and will continue to do so for as long as I allow it. Neither of them has ever learnt to create their own destiny and use their own creativity, and I failed to teach them that lesson by creating their destiny on their behalf and never discussing it with them. Why did I not discuss it with them? Because one has a bad temper and a vocabulary from the gutter whereas I like peace, and because the other is a very old friend that I thought I was helping.

I said what I did and did what I said, and in both instances, I ignored all the tiny signs that things were not going according to MY plan. I thought that both situations were only temporary, and therefore it was best for me to tolerate, be resilient and just live with it. The result was that I said what I did, but I in fact did not do what I said, because I did not want to experience a bad temper of disillusionment about a friendship. I did not live my own truth, and that is why I felt betrayed, angry and disappointed.

 Do you always say what you do and do what you say? What happens when you do?

I can aim these feelings at the other people who will probably continue their paths of destruction and self-destruction, or I can deal with my own feelings and accept that I did not live my own truth and am looking for someone to blame.

My challenge is to find the unconditional love that is there for these people and for everyone else. However, it does not need to be a challenge. I can simply find a way to lovingly voice my concerns, and move on. We like to think of it as a challenge when in fact unconditional love is our natural state. We still have so much to learn in this world.

21 I NOW DECLARE YOU ....

Why is it that so many relationships and marriages break up because of what one partner does or does not do? And even more puzzling: why is it that the villain gets into another relationship and becomes the perfect partner to a very happy person? Do people suddenly change their nature overnight?

And another puzzle: why is it that some people seem just unlucky in relationships? Serial spouses and celebrities with a string of broken relationships always make a good read in the popular magazines.

 Have you been in a relationship that did not work out? Why?

Maybe we need to look at these 'wrong' relationships with the 'wrong' people from a different angle.

What if these broken marriages and relationships are not 'wrong' choices? What if each one of them is a perfect choice, but we fail to see that, and judge ourselves as failures?

Let's take a step back and work from the assumption that we incarnated into this world because we have things to learn about ourselves. We have forgotten the reason why we are here: to live a life that will bring us closer to perfection and to the God that we were separated from.

We have become caught up in man-made and culture-based rules such as that people must be in a relationship for life, or that once married, divorce is a failure.

We have forgotten that our lives are pre-planned before we are born, and that we come here to live a perfectly designed script.

Am I saying that it is OK to flit from one relationship or marriage to another? Is it all right to have multiple partners throughout your life?

Maybe it is. What if your life script was designed so that you learn about yourself from having different relationships? And what if someone else's life script was designed so that they learn different lessons from the same partner over a much longer period?

We have been conditioned to focus on the 'failures' of relationships, rather than on the purpose of a relationship that has come to an end.

Because of this focus on 'failure', we do not allow ourselves or others the space to contemplate on what we have learnt from the relationship.

 What have you learnt from a love or friend relationship that did not last?

It is far easier to show interest in the gossip-worthy history of someone who 'failed' than to ask what they have learnt from the relationship about themselves.

We prefer to ask why the relationship has come to an end, and the reason behind the question is often to assign blame or to exonerate oneself. Our legal systems, religions and cultures have been designed to reinforce this issue of blaming others rather than understanding self.

Some people come out of a relationship, have clarity on what they want, and find the 'perfect' mate. They live happily ever after, but they have other lessons to learn, for example from experiences with colleagues at work or with their children or step-children.

Other people emerge from a relationship, refuse to do any introspection, and repeat the same pattern in subsequent relationships. And rather than encourage them to look at themselves in a loving way and become whole, we comment on their inability to have a stable relationship. That makes us as 'guilty' as they are. But we are all guilty of lacking insight - of nothing else.

We often see people being desperately unhappy in a relationship, but staying in it at all costs, and often against the advice of those who care about them. They stay because they are afraid of being by themselves rather than in a relationship. In some cultures, people stay in a sick relationship because of the social judgment that they will face when they leave, or more often because they simply don't understand what they need to deal with before they can leave the relationship.

Whatever the reason for remaining in a destructive relationship, or for having the same kind of relationship with different people over and over again, the bottom-line is that we need to understand the dynamic between the people in the relationship, and what there is to be learnt from it.

The important issue is not the destination, i.e. the end of the relationship, but rather the journey, i.e. the spiritual reason why we got involved in a relationship in the first place. Only then can we learn about ourselves and find peace and put the relationship behind us, with gratitude and love towards the person who helped us learn about ourselves, rather than with all the destructive feelings that we have learnt to associate with the end of a relationship.

22 HOW LONG SHOULD MARRIAGE VOWS LAST?

Any relationship has a natural duration, after which it ends – unless the people in the relationship hold on to the relationship for dear life.

This raises a question about marriage vows. Divorce statistics prove to us time and again that despite the religious and legal pressure on us, marriages do not last forever – they often do not even last for one lifetime.

And even where a marriage does last for a lifetime, people often tell me that they have been desperately unhappy in their 'long and happy' marriage because they were forced to stay in it for health or financial reasons or because of social pressure. In these situations, even though the marriage certificate is still in place, the marriage did not last for a lifetime. Who are we trying to fool?

 How long do you believe a marriage contract should last?

Why do we have marriage vows?

The earliest marriage vows were not between two people. The vows were between a person and a village that this person joined by means of a ceremony. The person undertook to help watch over and protect the tribe and the village, in exchange for their protection.

During the Middle Ages marriage vows became a legal contract between families. It was meant to protect the interests of the two families that were tied together by the union between a man and a woman. There was not necessarily a religious aspect to this.

Later, the church got involved and insisted on having a public ceremony where a couple made promises to each other 'until death do us part'. Sadly, there is so much religious pressure on many marriages that those words become the life-long sentence people have to live with – mostly emotional death, sometimes physical death. If you are still trapped in a marriage that has in all but the legal sense ended long ago, you will know what I am talking about.

Someone said to me the other day that even though he is divorced, he still believes that a marriage should last 'forever'. He said that when you get married, you do not decide whether you take the 10-year or the 15-year deal.

Of course, you don't, and even if you could, it would not make sense to choose any duration for the marriage in terms of time. The marriage - that is the relationship, regardless of its legal status - will endure for as long as the couple teaches each other what they undertook to do in their soul contracts which they entered before they were born.

The religious view on marriage vows has caused a lot of heart-ache, violence and emotional damage. People are expected to buy into the fantasy that a relationship will last 'forever'. When reality destroys the fantasy, the church and society heaps guilt onto the 'guilty' parties for failing to live up to the fantasy. When the relationship eventually ends – legally – too often the partners walk away with a sense of failure, rather than with a sense of achievement. This sense of failure in fact keeps them attached to the relationship well past its sell-by date.

Do we achieve anything from a broken relationship? Of course we do. We just do not acknowledge our achievements.

 What have you gained from a broken relationship?

I was married once, and I ended the marriage against much objection and prejudice after I had faced the wrong end of a fire-arm. I had to struggle for years with the guilt, sense of failure and programmed prejudice that was targeted at me and made my life one great misery.

Did I gain from the marriage and the divorce?

Of course I did. Even during my marriage, I had to rely on my own resources, and that made me realize that I was emotionally much stronger than anybody gave me credit for. I had to find solutions for problems that were not described in any textbook.

After my divorce, I was a 'sinner' and an outcast. That forced me to reach out to people who otherwise would have been off-limits to me for ridiculous reasons such as a different religion, language or marital status. I made great friends and learnt about unconditional Love.

When my 10-year-old son ran away from home in the night, I could not turn to anyone that I knew - not even my parents - to get help, because that would have provided proof of my failure as a single parent - which was anticipated all round as part of the culture I grew up in. It was part of the burden of being a divorced woman in an environment where the institution of marriage was (still is) worshipped.

At the time, I found my son within half an hour – and he was quite embarrassed and happy to be home again. That brought us closer and I learned to listen more to what he was saying, and also to what he was not saying – a skill that has been invaluable throughout my life.

When my boy discovered that he was becoming a father, he spontaneously told me that he was very happy to have me as 'the oracle on parenthood'. That was a humbling experience and it made more than twenty years of being a single parent worth every minute. Without my 'failed' marriage I would never have had that experience. And I can write a book about the other wonderful discoveries I have made about myself and other people over the years since I got divorced.

The Celtic hand-fasting ceremony is far more realistic than any religious marriage vows that I have encountered.

I will quote selectively from the vows that go with the hand-fasting ceremony:

"Will you cause him/her pain?

I May

Is that your intent?

No

Will you burden him/her?

I may

Is that your intent?

No

Will you cause him/her anger?

I may

Is that your intent?

No

Will you take the heat of anger and use it to temper the strength of this union?

We will.

The knots of this binding are not formed by these cords but instead by your vows. Either of you may drop the cords, for, as always, you hold in your own hands the making of breaking of this union."

These vows do not create any unrealistic expectations. They consider the fact that we are the masters of our own destinies, and that when things 'go wrong' there is not necessarily malicious intent. Life is about positive and negative experiences, and all these experiences are meant to provide balance.

And above all, the vows are not based on the assumption that 'failure' implies guilt. There is no such thing as failure. There is such a thing as being blind to the insights we are meant to gain from the relationship.

 If you ever had marriage vows, in which way did they fall short? In which way did you fall short?

The lessons we learn and the wisdom we gain from ending a relationship are eternal. The legal and religious paperwork attached to a relationship are not eternal. The guilt and sense of failure may be life-long, if you choose to hold on to that for the rest of your life.

23 ON MISTRESSES AND MORALS

I once shared a meal with some acquaintances. The conversation turned to how relationships start. Someone explained, amid much laughter from the group, how she tried everything to get away, but eventually realized that someone was Mr. Right and perfect for her. That moment changed her life.

One of the men nodded, and agreed that one just know when someone is right. He had the same feeling when he met his girlfriend a few months before.

I knew the man was married, but in England there is this weird situation where you get divorced in stages – like cutting off the tail of a dog bit by bit, so that it will hurt less? And from what I can gather British people generally do not wait for the process to end before they move on to a different relationship.

When I asked sympathetically how long the man had been separated from his wife, he said no, he is happily married. He then told me that in the UK it is 'traditional' for a man to have a mistress. He also said that his wife was aware of his 'lady friends' but she has no idea how intimate these 'friendships' are, and that kept them both happy.

 What are your views on extra-marital relationships?

That did not really surprise me. A few months after I moved to the UK, I went to visit a lady in her 80's when she was recovering in hospital after an operation. We were talking about the news of the day, which had something to do with the accident in which princess Diana died. I must have said something about Diana (I cannot remember the entire conversation) but that triggered a tirade against Diana because 'she did not know her place, she was not royal, and she complained about something that was nothing and embarrassed the royal family, because a man, and especially a prince, is fully entitled to his 'bit on the side' '.

I was astonished at the time, not so much about what the old lady said, but because I got to know her as a person with Christian views and a staunch supporter of the Church of England. But then the Church of England has its roots in the actions of King Henry VIII who had a wandering eye and believed that his rules were the only valid rules, especially when it came to women.

I was not quite sure what to think about this man who seemed to be an intelligent, decent man who got on well with everybody. You would think that he is a predator who finds vulnerable women, tells them that he is married and intends to remain so, and then has a relationship with them that obviously excludes children and many other means of sharing a life. Those women know that they cannot make any claim on his time or how he lives his life, because society will turn against the women as being home-wreckers. Few people will question the motives of a happily married man.

I am not convinced that his wife really knows nothing about these other women (it turned out there were two of them at the time, and he really had to juggle his social schedule to get around to everyone and ensure that he is not discovered).

Is this about morality? That is what most people would think.

However, I am convinced that it is about balance. The husband finds other women because he is missing something in his life. He does not have much in common with his wife (I overheard conversations where he was perfectly civil and friendly with her, but he could not remember on which day of the week she has a half-day job). This does not matter to him because by the time he gets home she is there, waiting for him. With his mistresses, on the other hand, he always knows where they are – and this is important because he does not want them to run into each other or into his wife. That is balance.

Where is the balance for the wife? She is financially dependent on her husband. If she leaves him, she will have to find a job to maintain herself. If she values having loads of free time without her husband (that may even include a relationship with another man) and being maintained by a man, then she is satisfied. However, this will only be the position when she values those money and freedom above fidelity and honesty.

Where is the balance for the mistress? Her need for sex is satisfied, and she has the excitement of an illicit relationship as well as companionship. At the same time, she has an admirer who is not there all the time, which gives her freedom. As long as these values outrank the values of, for example, having children or a relationship based on trust, then she is happy.

Most often when a relationship comes to an end, it is because the values of the two partners clash. Sometimes people get into a relationship with conflicting values, and they quickly move from infatuation to resentment and eventually the end of the relationship. Other times people with different values have a relationship, and they grow and learn from one another.

When you consider the satisfaction of values in a marriage rather than at the document that makes it a marriage, the picture looks different. And the same holds for other relationships like employment or friendship as well.

Next time I will withhold my judgment and rather add to my understanding.

 In your experience, what do people gain or lose from extra-marital relationships?

24 BIGAMY DOES NOT UNDERMINE THE INSTITUTION OF MARRIAGE

I can feel just this title is enough cause for me to duck some eggs, oranges and other missiles, but your actions would be uninformed, so let's have a truce while I state my case.

A woman was sentenced to ten months in prison, suspended for two years, for 'marrying' four men while she was still married to her first husband. She was cautioned by police for two of these illegal marriages, and spent six months in prison for one of them. Despite all this, she went ahead and 'married' a fifth man who discovered his place in the pecking order while they were on honeymoon.

This woman was twelve years old when she persuaded her parents to buy her first wedding dress, and got married to her first husband when she was eighteen.

When she was sentenced, the judge claimed that her actions 'undermine the institution of marriage'. This is where I disagree. I believe she exposed the institution of marriage for what it has become, and nobody is listening.

 What are your views on marriage?

I believe any legal actions which are based on the institution of marriage in fact undermine marriage. Marriage is a contract of love between two people. The legal contract has over hundreds of years become so deeply ingrained as a means of solidifying things other than love that we have lost focus.

In many cultures, marriage has been a financial bargaining tool, and to this day men in some cultures are expected to pay a dowry when they 'buy' a bride. Marriage has also become a means of tying dynasties together, as we still see in royal or wealthy circles.

Marriage has also become a legal means of managing property, as we see every day in prenuptial agreements, marriage contracts and divorce settlements.

The wedding ceremony became part of a strategy for ingraining religious fear and control, and some cultures still have a strong censorship against people who have relationships outside of marriage. There are people who cannot imagine a worse future than marrying outside of their religion. They chose one version of faith as the be-all and end-all, and are too afraid to consider any possibility of falling in love with someone who does not accept such man-made limitations.

Many people choose to have no sex before marriage, and expect to be treated as modern-day martyrs for their stance. Yes, stay away from sex until you are absolutely sure you can emotionally commit to a sexual relationship – this will ensure you make an informed choice based on love rather than hormones.

 What are your views on sex before marriage? Why?

But does a marriage certificate guarantee a satisfying sexual relationship? Many people would tell you the opposite – or would they rather keep quiet about their sexual failure or incompatibility because it is not acceptable to openly discuss the true motivation for two people joining in marriage, namely love? A wise man once told me that where a marriage relationship is solid and healthy, sex forms 5% of the relationship. However, where the relationship is rocky sex forms 95% of the relationship. If you insist on waiting for sex after marriage, maybe you are focusing in the wrong place and heading for disillusion?

For some religions marriage no longer provides the opportunity to manipulate people who choose to have a strong love relationship without the massive expense that a wedding ceremony requires. One religious group recently attempted to get some of the control back by offering a bargain price combination of marriage for parents and baptism for their children at a discount. If those people wanted to succumb to the pressure of the church to control their lives, surely they would have done so before they had children?

All the above actions undermine the institution of marriage, which should be a union of love (with witnesses and paperwork that confirms love rather than a legal cover-your-backside for future actions).

This bigamous woman probably has serious relationship issues that she brought with her from one or more previous lives as part of the blueprint for her life. Her sacral chakra may be completely out of balance, which means she will keep searching for a secure relationship but not understand what she wants or why she is never satisfied with a partner. She may have serious relationship issues stemming from incidents in her childhood where she formed a perception which are still impacting on her decisions and actions. She may have brought unresolved memories from previous lives with her. The lithium that apparently has been prescribed to her will not neutralize any of these issues.

Did she undermine the institution of marriage? Or did she get people to question their own beliefs and perceptions? Did she get spiritual support on resolving her relationship issues and growing towards wholeness? Or was she punished for not toeing the line or 'playing the game'?

Nothing prevents her from having a string of relationships without getting married – she had boyfriends in between her fake marriages and was not punished by law for any of those.

However, she chose to rock the boat by having sham marriages, and her environment responded by punishing her rather than questioning to what extent the marriage ceremony has been degraded to a means of manipulation rather than a union of love.

When you initially read the title of this article, did you react because you wanted to protect your union of love, or because you reacted to fear of shaking up your own beliefs in case I have a point?

25 LETTING GO OF A RELATIONSHIP

Why is it that we hold on to relationships long past their natural end?

 What relationship are you holding on to against your better judgment?

Think of a friendship that no longer exists. Do you still remember how your friend insulted or deserted you? You gained new friends, but you still feel that hurt.

Remember that supervisor who made your life such hell that you left to get a new job? You smile every time you think what a sad sod that supervisor is, and how much better off you are now. Or you still resent the opportunity that you missed because of that person, even though you gained much more from the new job than from the old one.

Then of course there is your marriage. You have known for a long time that there is nothing left of that relationship, but you still hold on. You cannot get a divorce – or so you have convinced yourself. You are dying a slow death every day because your partner refuses to change.

Probably the most destructive relationship to hold on to is a marriage, because of all the social and cultural restrictions against divorce. Somehow, we share a belief that a marriage must last forever, even if statistics confirm that most marriages do not last forever.

If you end a marriage, does that mean your relationship has failed? That depends on what you take away from the marriage.

Let's assume that you decided to end the marriage because you discovered your partner is cheating on you. Of course, the cheating partner is wrong and should carry all the blame. Or maybe not?

Let us take a step back and look at the situation from a different angle.

You had expectations of the relationship. You made those expectations clear to your partner, who obliged and lived up to your expectations.

Everyone was happy and all was well. You were very pleased with yourself.

Then you discovered that your partner was seeing someone else. This of course was devastating. When you confronted your partner, they had nothing to say, or they said 'it did not really mean anything', or they said 'you won't understand'.

Did you listen to that? Did you hear what your cheating partner was saying to you?

 Looking back at a failed relationship, what did you gain from it?

It is not pleasant to realize that the relationship was all about you and your expectations. It takes much effort and sometimes a large leap of courage to look at the face in the mirror and see who carries 50% of the 'blame' for a relationship where one person cheated.

Cheating is only the symptom of the lack of communication in the relationship. Did you ever listen to your partner? Did you ever ask and discover what your partner really values?

Of course, it is quite disappointing to discover that a person does not live up to your expectations. But in any relationship, there are two people and they both have expectations. One person may have the vocabulary to express their expectations and values, while another person uses their behavior to express their expectations and values.

Who is wrong? The person who is 'wrong' is not the one who cheated. The person who is 'wrong' is the one who does not at the end of a relationship step back and do some introspection.

What did you learn from this partner? In what way did you grow from the relationship? What was the most valuable thing you gained from the relationship? How did the relationship make you wiser and stronger? In what way was your partner the best teacher you could ever have had to learn that specific lesson?

Life is about balance. For every light side, there is a dark side. And this is the blatantly obvious bit that we like to overlook: for every dark side there is also a light side.

The closer we get to the natural completion of a relationship, the more we focus on the dark side and the hurt from the relationship. This hurt gets so intense that we completely forget to look for the light side – the gain from the relationship.

Often a relationship ends on the surface, but that does not mean we get closer to the natural completion. Think about divorces where the hurt and pain drags on throughout the divorce negotiations – and often for years afterwards, long after the divorce was finalized.

Are you still in some way holding on to a failed relationship, when you should have left it behind years ago?

As long as we get stuck on the part of the equation that focuses on 'me, myself and I' and 'the things they did to me', the relationship drags on.

Dealing with the paperwork or dividing possessions does not end a relationship. Getting into another, more fulfilling, loving relationship does not end a relationship.

The only way to end a relationship is to acknowledge how that relationship changed you for the better, and then to thank your partner for being a valuable part of the experience. Then let go of the relationship and hold on to the learning experience.

Yes, it is possible to thank any partner for their contribution to your growth, even if the partner raped or abused you, or was an addict. You had that experience - not so that it would destroy you, but so that it would help you heal a division inside of yourself.

The secret of gaining from ending a relationship is to acknowledge the nature of that division, and to move from being divided to wholeness, gratitude and Love.

As long as you hold on to the division and look for someone to blame for your hurt, you will remain divided, hurt and in a dark place. Understanding yourself comes in small portions. Accept the small portions and grow from them.

 In what way did a failed relationship make you more whole?

On a lighter note: A doctor addressing a large audience said: "The material we put into our stomachs is enough to have killed most of us sitting here, years ago. Red meat is awful. Soft drinks corrode your stomach lining. Chinese food is loaded with MSG. High fat diets can be disastrous, and none of us realizes the long-term harm caused by the germs in our drinking water.

But there is one thing that is the most dangerous of all and we all have, or will, eat it.

Can anyone here tell me what food it is that causes the most grief and suffering for years after eating it?"

After several seconds of quiet, a 75-year-old man in the front row raised his hand, and softly said 'Wedding Cake.'

26 HOW CAN YOU DO THIS TO ME?

Some people are real suckers for punishment. Like those women that keep going back to partners that abuse them physically and verbally. And there are men as well that stay with abusive partners, or people who stay in jobs or in friendships where they are bullied.

No, I am not judging them. I also have a lot of empathy for them, because it took me years to shake off some abusive relationships, many destructive work environments and some feel-bad friendships, even after I had recognized what was happening. I was also a sucker for punishment.

In this case, there is more truth in that expression - 'sucker for punishment' - than we may realize.

We are all One and part of the same perfect diamond that is called God – or any other name that you know Him/Her by. All of us are required to form this perfect diamond, and the diamond would be flawed if any one of us is different or missing. Abusers also form part of the same diamond, and they are also part of our Oneness.

When we are in any type of relationship with a person, we have an additional bond with that person – over and above the one we have with all humanity. Imagine that bond to be like a very strong silver cord that ties two people together. That cord exists between the abuser and the abused, just like it exists between two married people who have been in a happy relationship for forty or more years.

We enter relationships because we know intuitively that we need the other person to learn important things about ourselves, and to help us get a balance in ourselves that we would otherwise miss.

 Who is the person who treated you worst in a failed love or friendship relationship? What did you learn from it about yourself?

Why would anyone willingly enter an abusive relationship? Even when people close to you warn you of what they can see but you cannot? And why would anyone stay in that relationship even when their physical and emotional safety is on line?

Because we are 'suckers for punishment'. That silver cord is firmly in place, and it literally sucks us back to the other person until we either realize that we no longer need them and move on, or until there is an incident that weighs more than the pull from that cord, for example when our lives are threatened.

All the time while the cord is in place and we stay in an abusive relationship, we hand our own personal power over to the other person. That cord is based in the solar plexus chakra, where our will power is seated.

When the solar plexus chakra is open and healthy, we understand that we are in charge of our own lives and that we can make our own decisions. We then contribute to a relationship in equal measures, and we understand that we are in the first place individuals, and in the second place part of a relationship.

When the solar plexus chakra is blocked and not healthy, we often believe that we are powerless and that we must just suffer the punishment that is meted out to us by our partners – or even by work colleagues or other family members that abuse us. The silver cord ties us to those people as well and not just to partners in a love relationship.

That is why people tend to stay in an abusive relationship for long times, and why they often go back even when they do get the courage to move out. They are pulled back by this cord that ties them to the abuser, because physical distance from an abuser does not change the belief that they are powerless. Physical distance does not stop them handing their power over to the abuser, because physical distance is a man-made concept and not real. That silver cord is real.

Once the change happens in the person and he/she starts to understand that they have a personal power and they take that power back, the solar plexus chakra starts to function normally. Then the person gets the courage to leave the relationship. This could mean getting a divorce, changing jobs if the abuser is a work colleague, or breaking off ties – yes, that is literally what happens – with an abusive friend or family member.

Sometimes that realization of having personal power takes a very long time, and we are forcibly removed from the situation, for example we face the wrong end of a fire-arm and flee to safety, and that gives us the courage to stay away from the abuser and heal the solar plexus chakra. Or we get dismissed from a job and discover that we are better off in a different job. Even then, it could take years to find our balance again.

The question is: why is this kind of information not available to us when we most need it? Why is the understanding and the healing not available much earlier?

I suppose that is where our karma comes in — we need the experiences to find a balance with previous experiences. We choose our lives and our experiences, and at times it is hard to remember that all our experiences and our entire lives are perfect for our purpose in this life.

 Looking back at past relationships, what do you feel grateful for?

27 LOVE AND MARRIAGE

We like ceremonies and celebrations. We scoff at ceremonies like coronations, inaugurations, society weddings and other public celebrations, but only after we had watched them, so that we can ridicule the detail. We silently place ourselves in the place of the main characters in the celebration, and wish for our own turn.

I remember when Prince Charles and Princess Diana got married. At the time, I was working as a civil servant in South Africa. For one day, we were allowed to break all the rules. I had a portable television set in my office, and we gathered around it all day so that we would not miss even a tiny detail of the broadcast. This was years after South Africa became a republic, and we had no official ties with the royal family. It did not matter. We were caught up in the magic.

I recently heard about a man who spent that entire day in bed with his girlfriend, now his wife of many years. They obviously had their own magic going on that day.

In England, the expression "getting a hat" means that a couple has decided to get married and it is time to prepare for a celebration, part of which is to buy a hat to wear to the ceremony.

Nowadays a wedding is preceded by months of planning and huge expenses. Everything must be just right, and there are even mock weddings before the day so that every participant can remember their steps for the big moment.

Sadly, the cost of a traditional wedding and the emphasis on the legal aspects of the wedding put people off the idea of marriage. Add to that the high divorce rate and the negative emotions that go with divorce, and marriage becomes a lot less attractive.

How important is marriage for you? Why?

The gagirl (http://www.gagirl.com/wedding/wedding2.html) website contains a lot of amusing and eye-opening information about the various traditions that go with the modern Christian wedding ceremony. Virtually nothing of the ceremony has anything to do with being Christian – or belonging to any other faith group.

Considering that marriage is not even mentioned in the Bible (except for some oblique reference by Paul), it is interesting how much emphasis the churches and even some governments place on the institution of the Christian marriage as a means of controlling relationships.

Among all the fuss, we miss the point. Does it really matter what style the wedding dress is or which side the groom stands on? What difference will the honeymoon destination make to the ceremony, except to cause stress when the couple is probably already not quite keeping up with expectations?

What is far more important is the celebration of joy and happiness when two people find each other and decide to be a couple. And that does not need to be celebrated with pomp and ceremony.

 How would you choose to celebrate joy and happiness with a Love partner?

There is the modern practice of dating many people and having no-strings-attached sex with various partners. As a friend of mine once put it, there is nothing wrong with good, happy, healthy sex, no matter who your partner is. That would not work for me, but who are we to judge one another? I once read somewhere a very cynical definition of love: when two people wake up together in the same bed in the morning and neither wants to leave, they have found love. Such occasions probably call for a minor celebration, but I wonder.

On the other hand, we have all seen couples that are radiant together. They clearly belong together and they want the world to know this. Now that is a celebration. I mean, every time they are in the presence of others and their happiness spill over to other people, there is a celebration of love. Whether they ever get married or not becomes irrelevant.

I once had a colleague who had that kind of love with her husband. They both had successful careers and they had two lovely children. Because of discriminatory tax legislation, they had to pay a huge penalty for being married and successful. They got divorced and did not tell anybody. She confided in me a few years after the divorce and I wondered how she could be so matter-of-fact about this. This was when my own acrimonious divorce was still fresh in my mind.

Then she invited me to their house and I met her husband – and all became clear to me. They had been together for nearly thirty years, and they were still in love and acting like newly-weds. There were moments when nobody else existed for them in the room. I realized that what they had was a meeting of souls, and that the angels celebrate with them every time they are together. That is when I put in my order for a similar relationship.

The union of two souls is a celebration. Does it matter whether the union is between a man and a woman, or between two people of the same sex in a relationship? Not for me.

And this union does not only happen between couples. I have seen the same thing with a teenage girl holding her mother's hand in the company of other adults. The girl was a stunningly beautiful, well-adjusted young lady who was quite comfortable with expressing her obvious love for her mother in this way.

I have seen two sisters - quite different in nature - embrace each other for no specific reason. And that was not a once-off occasion. Those sisters are both married women today and will still walk through the proverbial fire for each other.

I had a friend who shared my path with me for over twenty years. We lived in different countries, grew up in vastly different cultures, and she smoked like a chimney, but I was with her when she waded through hell and she had been there for me during my worst and best times, often without question, sometimes with strong criticism, but always with love. The bond between us transcended all differences, and our differences enriched our friendship to the end.

And I am fortunate enough to often associate with kindred spirits that radiate this kind of love. Namaste to all my free flying friends out there!

No document or ceremony can capture this kind of love, and when it happens to you, you will know, because the room will be full of angels. When you find such love, hold on to it.

 Have you ever experienced a Love for another person that transcended everything else?

28 UNHAPPY FAMILIES ARE A BLESSING

I recently read a fascinating book about *Henry VIII* (http://www.amazon.co.uk/dp/0099437244/ref=nosim?tag=wwwmypurpl ebl-21) and his six wives. The author of the book states that happy families all resemble one another, while unhappy families are unhappy in their own unique ways.

 Are you from a happy family with no challenges?

And Henry VIII was very good at creating unique unhappy families. He was married six times. During an age where divorce was the last option and the divorce of a monarch was unthinkable, he divorced his first wife, had the second one beheaded, lost the third in child-birth, divorced number four, had number five beheaded and left number six widowed.

I recently attended a talk where the presenters described their upbringing to give some perspective to their product. They started the presentation by asking the audience how many people were from dysfunctional families. As you could expect, some hands went up immediately (some people like to define themselves by means of their history rather than who they really are) and other hands went up reluctantly (because we all have some skeletons in our closets).

The one presenter then said 'As I expected – we are all from dysfunctional families' as if that was a given. It became clear during their presentation that their view of the world being populated by dysfunctional families impacted on everything they had personally experienced.

It reminded me again that we like to put labels on people, because it makes us feel safe. We tend to compare ourselves to other people, see their challenges in life and then see our own challenges in a far better light.

You may have heard about the woman who discovered that her husband was having an affair. They moved in circles where this happened quite often, but people were very discrete about it. However, this woman was determined not to share her husband.

She confronted her husband with the evidence, and he calmly acknowledged that he was having an affair with a woman. He reminded her that his friend Bob had been having an affair for years, that she was aware of it and never had an issue with it.

However, the wife would not tolerate her own husband having an affair, and of course she then threatened to divorce him if he did not end the affair immediately.

His response was 'OK, you can have a divorce. You will also have your credit card taken away from you, which means you will have to get a job. You will no longer get a new car every two years or holidays on tropical islands once a year. You will not be able to buy designer clothes or get your regular beauty treatments. Would you really like a divorce?'

The wife thought about this for a while, and then said 'I think our mistress is far more beautiful than Bob's.'

 Have you ever needed to confronted the reality that is offered here as a joke? How would or did you deal with it?

On a more serious note, the reasons why families are 'dysfunctional' or challenging are because they teach us things about ourselves. We choose our families before we enter this existence because our interaction with them highlights our own needs for spiritual growth. Somehow, we allow families to get away with behavior that we would definitely not tolerate from others. We do this because we intuitively know our families love us and will always love us no matter what. We tolerate their actions until we have learnt what we needed to learn from them, and once we understand our love for them only becomes deeper.

Some people thrive on their badges of being from dysfunctional families. That blurs their own perceptions, but that is also part of their journeys.

I know of a couple who were both abandoned as babies. The husband was from a large family, and he was given away to an unmarried aunt who had a no children but a very strong maternal drive – so strong that she in fact emotionally abused the boy. By the age of about ten, he was claimed back by his mother. You can imagine the impact this upbringing had on him.

The wife was given to her grandparents when she was a baby, because both parents had serious health problems. She grew up thinking that her grandparents were her parents, until she was six years old. She had no contact with her biological parents and did not even know that they were alive. Then her parents simply appeared one day and claimed her back and took her home with them. Imagine the impact this had on the little girl, being taken away from a familiar environment and having to get used to two complete strangers who were now the new figures of authority in her life.

These two people then married and had a daughter. The daughter became anorexic and suicidal in her teens and nearly ruined her parents financially and emotionally with her excessive demands for things and situations that could potentially make her happy and stop her torturing herself and her parents.

The parents liked to describe the whole experience as an intervention from the Holy Spirit to help them realize that money and earthly possessions are not important. They described their daughter as a 'very mature teacher' of spiritual lessons.

My view was that they were both abandoned as children, and then overcompensated with their child's upbringing by smothering her with their version of parental love. They did everything they could to give her the opposite of the childhood they had. The daughter then rebelled by becoming anorexic and by playing on their guilt feelings and manipulating them to the hilt.

How would they react to a different view on their experiences? Would they sit up and think about it and learn even more about their journey? Would they reject a view that clashes with their view of the world and continue to miss the point? Or is this a point I want to make based on my ignorance? After all, I was not there and heard their version of the events long after they took place.

And those are the questions that each of us – at least those that do come from unhappy families- must ask of ourselves.

 Have you gained in any way by coming from s dysfunctional family? How?

Being a member of an unhappy family is a challenge because our relatives remind us time and again of our own dark sides. Because it is a challenge, we tend to prefer the least painful perspective on the issue.

How would each of us react to a view of our lives that focuses on the pain? Would we understand that the healing will only take place once we experience an equal amount of pain and pleasure, and achieve a balanced perspective on our experiences?

Confronting our own dark side is a brave act. We often choose to gloss over it, or wear it as a 'badge of injury' rather than deal with it.

Once we start to search for the advantages in the experiences that shaped us, we gain an understanding of where and how it fits into the Master Plan. We see that every single experience has a positive and a negative side. We stop focusing on the negative side and get a balanced view. Only then can we experience gratitude and get a feeling of the immense Love that God has for us. That is the moment where our lives really begin.

And that is the moment when a dysfunctional family begins to heal and start to see and love the lighter side of one another.

29 I NEED A DIVORCE – AND QUICKLY

What do you do when you let your heart run free, knowing even as it happens that you have made the worst possible decision? We often hear about celebrities who get married on a whim, and within a matter of days, or sometimes weeks, they head for the divorce court. They have the courage to stand up in public and say 'This is not for me.'

But many people do not end a spur-of-the moment marriage so quickly. They decide to make the best of it, to work on the relationship, to sleep in the bed that they have made for themselves, and so on and so on.

Which is the best way to go? Get out of the marriage quickly, or work on it? There is no right or wrong answer. The issue does get confused when a marriage certificate is brought in, because then there are legal as well as emotional ties that need to be cut.

 Do you know anyone who got married for the wrong reasons and then regretted it? How did they deal with it? How would you have dealt with it?

Some people get married based on passion – and passion invariably burns out when the reality of daily life makes demands. When the lid of the toothpaste tube is missing, or when an unexpectedly large bill is to be paid, or the toilet seat is up, or the pockets of the clothes in the laundry bag have not been emptied, a minor incident could become a stone in a shoe and eventually a reason for divorce.

But then these issues are superficial and only become serious when they are symptoms of other, more deep-rooted issues. Often a failed marriage is based on unrealistic expectations. The ideal is to enter the marriage with no expectations at all, but we often live in a culture where especially marriage comes with many unrealistic expectations.

A comedian once said that a bride's attitude towards her betrothed can be summed up in three words: Isle. Altar. Hymn. The implication is that women enter a marriage with the expectation that she will get her way, but at times men also do this.

 Can you change the nature or habits of another person to make you happy?

Either way, we miss the point here. A marriage or a wedding is not about the ceremony or about the legalities. It is always about the lessons that people must learn from each other. There is no such thing as a mistake or a wrong decision. Some decisions have consequences that are harder to deal with, but those decisions are the ones that we learn most from about ourselves.

Some of us have entered a marriage or other relationship, even an employment relationship, knowing in the pit of our stomachs that we make the biggest possible mistake, and at the same time knowing that there is no turning back. We then spent much energy first 'working on the relationship', and then justifying why we are in it.

When the right answers do not come, we get angry at the world, and if we are willing to take responsibility for our actions, we get angry at ourselves for being so stupid.

The next step of this completely natural process is to get depressed – depression is anger without passion. Only then do we get the courage to make the required change and get out of the relationship.

The aftermath of such an experience is often that we spend a long time in turmoil and going through all these emotions again and again. Some people never get the point, while others get the point and move on.

What is the point? It is that we go through these experiences because they are meant to teach us about ourselves. We have work or love relationships with these people because they had agreed to become our teachers. Often these decisions are meant for us to experience our dark sides – where we must confront our own demons – and the partners in these relationships help us to do this.

When we do not understand how these experiences shape us, we get stuck in the turmoil of 'how could they do that to me' or 'how could I have been so stupid'.

 Do you understand why you needed to put a relationship behind you? Have you moved on?

However, when the moment of understanding happens, we feel such immense relief. That is the moment when we see the actions of the other person in perspective, not as vindictive, but rather as a means of helping us to get our own demons out in the open.

That is the moment when we grow up and experience gratitude. We can then go back to the people who have 'done these things to us' and thank them for their contribution to our inner peace.

Imagine a society where we understand that all experiences are learning experiences. We are far from it yet. What we do have is a society that seeks to blame and to place the burden of our own lack of self-insight on other people.

Of course, we can allow these various emotions to get out of hand, and take some rash action. For example, there was the woman who approached the local pharmacist and asked for cyanide. 'What on earth would you want to do with cyanide?' he asked.

'I want to poison my husband' she said coolly.

Of course, the pharmacist was quite upset about this and made it quite clear to her that he was not going to be part of such a plot, and that he had no intention of selling any poison to her for that purpose.

The woman then took a photograph out of her bag. It showed the pharmacist's wife in bed with the woman's husband.

'Now that changes the situation,' the pharmacist said. 'You did not tell me that you had a prescription.'

30 YOU CANNOT MAKE ANYONE LOVE YOU

Why is it that some women find it so difficult to let go of a man who is not interested in a relationship with them?

I often speak to women who have their eye on a man who is not responsive. These women will do anything to get the man to respond to them. They will think about him all the time, and even send him long emails and regular text messages. When they get no response or a non-committal response, they look for ways to make the man love them.

Most of the time these women don't want to hear that the man is not interested in a relationship with them - and often not even in a friendship.

And the poor man cannot run away fast or far enough. Often their only 'sin' was a friendly greeting or an innocent compliment.

 Do you know a woman who is so desperate for a relationship that she would harass a man? Does it work for her?

When a man says 'you look beautiful today', it is not a marriage proposal. It is also not the beginning of a relationship. It is often not even interest in you as a potential partner. It is just a bit of flattery.

When a woman regards the most insignificant attention from a man as the beginning of something serious, that woman needs to ask herself why she so desperately needs attention and confirmation from someone else to establish her self-worth.

Even in our enlightened age men don't like to be the prey. A small handful of men are egotistic enough to enjoy the attention, but even these men feel crowded soon enough.

In one instance a woman told me that she knew the man was going to marry her, because even though they had not had contact for over ten years, she is convinced of their 'spiritual connection'.

I have no doubt that such a 'spiritual connection' exists between these women and the men who spend much energy evading them.

Sadly, the connection is one-sided – the woman fixates on the man and gets all her energy from him. This must leave the man tired for no obvious reason, because he may not be consciously aware of the woman using him as a source of energy.

I always ensure that any guidance I give to clients is honest and responsible. It is immensely frustrating to deal with clients who do not hear a word I am saying, and who want to blame me for not helping them to get any interest from the man.

If such clients then leave me because I did not tell them what they wanted to hear, I count my blessings. To me it means that they will not use me as a source of energy, and I can help other people.

If a woman needs to get her energy from another person, she also needs to work on her self-belief. We all can generate our own energy and share it with others. Where a woman believes that she is not capable of generating her own energy, she often suppresses the energy that she has. This makes her less creative, and such energy blockages can result in dis-ease of the female reproductive systems.

I have seen countless instances where such women discovered their own strength outside of a relationship and then had a lovely relationship with a man who wanted to be with them. Such an equal partnership works far better than a predator-prey situation which eventually results in energy blockages in both partners.

If you are waiting for a specific man to show some fleeting interest in you again, my recommendation is to forget him, and find an interesting hobby to spend your time and energy on.

Before you know it, you will be pursued and wooed for the interesting person you are, rather than be avoided for the desperate person you were.

31 BEWARE OF A FAMILY WITHOUT DIFFERENCES

Are you fed up with conflict in your family? Do you want everyone to have peace? Read this article and discover how a peaceful family could in fact be a dysfunctional family.

A wise man once said that if you have a family with no strife, no issues, no conflict, you should be seriously concerned about the state of affairs.

This was brought home to me again when I asked about the feeding of my grand-daughter – was it breast or bottle? I deliberately asked the question because I wanted to encourage the mother to exercise her personal choice. I believe that a mother instinctively knows what is good for her and her baby.

I recently heard about a matriarch – a mother of five (including twins) and grandmother of a handful – who is regarded as the oracle on motherhood, and nobody in her family would dare contradict her on how to raise a child. She had obviously missed the point that no two children are the same, unless you wear blinkers.

When a recent great-grandchild arrived, this oracle of motherhood insisted that the baby had to be breastfed. As a result, the poor new mother was forced to sit with the new baby for seven hours so that she could learn to breastfeed.

Can you imagine that anyone can be so cruel and destructive? This matriarch likes to brag about how tight-knit her family is, and how they gather around her for all high days and holidays. Whenever a decision needs to be made by a child, the oracle is consulted – or rather they approach the matriarch for her verdict, which is followed to the letter, for fear of the consequences.

One person dared to contradict her and refused to follow her instructions, and was 'excommunicated' on the spot and ignored by the rest of the family who are victims of mass hypnosis and would never question the judgment of the matriarch.

 Who is the most powerful person in your family? How do you deal with that person?

Then rather give me a family where the characters and their likes and dislikes are miles apart. I love to meet with my siblings whenever I can. We think in different ways, we have developed different cultures in our immediate families, and we represent extremes. This means we always have something to explore, and our arguments always end in love and understanding.

Every family needs balance, and you cannot possibly have balance when everyone sits on the same side of the see-saw. When the matriarch sits on the high side of the see-saw and the rest of the family sits in worship on the low side of the see-saw, there is no balance.

The only way for that family to have any balance, is to have a common 'enemy' which is the rest of the world. Anyone who dares to say that for example breastfeeding is one option rather than the only possibility becomes part of the common enemy. Where a family agrees on everything, I would wonder whether the family is really a healthy family.

Please remember to appreciate and love your family because they are different from you.

32 HOW DO YOU BOND WITH YOUR LOVED ONES?

I am fascinated by all the myths around bonding between people – not only parents and children, but also friends.

One myth is that a mother has difficulty bonding with a baby after a caesarean section. Another one is that all parents must bond with their children, or they risk being branded as bad parents.

What is this bonding? For me it is a feeling of 'knowing' a person. You know that the person resonates with you and you want to be in their presence, or you know that the person is bad news for you and you do not want to be in their presence. This has nothing to do with family ties. It has everything to do with the energy vibration that we all exude.

I once experienced a feeling of repulsion with a new-born baby for no reason at all. Over the years that baby turned into an attractive, intelligent young person who has always treated me well, but that did not do anything to dissolve that feeling of me wanting to run away when I am in the presence of that person, despite my best sermons to myself about Loving thy neighbor.

 Have you ever felt an irrational dislike for a person for no reason? How do you manage it without making the situation worse?

I recently talked to someone who feels a similar sense of repulsion for a young person that I get on well with. I was not sure which was worse – the disgust for a well-educated, well-groomed but slightly overconfident teenager, or the self-disgust because they could not find a logical reason for their dislike of the person.

There is no rule that says people must love their children. It is quite possible to have a child and not like the child, even when they are new-born babies.

Sometimes people can justify their dislike. For example, my mother was quite disgusted to find herself at the age of 18 with a baby who destroyed all her dreams of achieving something in her life. Of course, she was quite brilliant and had all the opportunity to achieve her dreams at a later age, but she chose to fixate her emotions on me (the baby) and blame me for being born and destroying her life.

She did not feel the same brooding anger towards my siblings, because in her mind the damage was done when I was conceived, and there was no reason to blame my siblings for the damage that my presence did.

I grew up knowing that my mother did not love me – she did not even like me, despite my best efforts. She saw all my achievements as a threat to her dwindling dreams, and when I did not achieve she found the proverbial stick to beat me up with for being lazy. No matter what I did, I could not win and the emotional abuse never stopped.

I was well into my thirties before I realized that nothing I could say, think or do would make her change her mind about me. By that time, she was an alcoholic and drug addict, and whenever she went for another unsuccessful treatment, I got the dreaded phone call from the health care professional about my "cruelty" towards my mother – while I just felt incredible sadness and confusion about the situation.

After my mother's death, I knew I had to make peace with the memory of being unwanted. The alternative was to label myself as "I am Elsabe and I was an unwanted child". Thank goodness, I realized that the way she treated me resulted in me finding my worth inside of myself rather than in the approval of others. It took me years to look at the face in the mirror, and even more years to learn and later love that face and that person. This is not a narcissistic self-admiration, but rather self-acceptance and getting comfortable in my own skin despite how other people treat me.

 Have you ever been rejected by a person who should have loved you? How did you manage it?

When you look at the way waves of different frequencies react when they collide in nature, you will realize that some waves fit together perfectly because they share the same wave-length. Other waves clash and the result is fragmentation and chaos.

People consist of energy, and we also respond like waves. With some people, you communicate easily because you are 'on the same wave-length'. With other people, you clash because you share incompatible frequencies. The behaviors of people are no different from the behavior of energy waves in nature, because people consist of energy waves.

The difference with people is that we have agendas for our existence here. When we clash with people, their agenda is to help us make peace with those parts of ourselves that we disown. They have this agenda because it is part of the contract that we enter with various people before we incarnate.

This is what works for me: when I discover that a person does not resonate with me, I grin and bear it until I can put into words what it is that I find repulsive about the person. Then I do introspection until I am clear in my mind on exactly how and when I display that same repulsive trait. This does not suddenly mean I discover an unconditional love for the person and we get on well from there onwards. It does mean that I understand what it is that I need to accept in myself, and that I am reminded of any residue of self-rejection every time I meet with that person.

Whenever I discover and accept another part of that self-disgust that is reflected in the other person, a quantum of light is formed and my own bodily vibration changes to a higher frequency. Rather than outright rejection, I am then able to display tolerance towards that person.

If life was uncomplicated, we would not have bothered living on this planet.

33 A SENSE OF BELONGING

I am very fortunate in that I am part of a large family. My dad was the eldest of eight children, and he had four children and four step-children himself.

I recently attended one of those occasions that bring large families together – a funeral. What struck me most is how the younger generation, my cousins, nephews and nieces, navigate artificial boundaries such as religious differences, cultural habits, and even time and space. I had not seen many of the relatives in more than 15 years, but there was a Love and goodwill that transcended everything.

This Love was not only part of mourning – it was preceded by relatives tracing each other on Facebook and discovering the interesting people behind the memories and photographs. We are always at the back of each other's minds, because we are truly connected.

This occasion was also preceded by a time of dealing with serious illness and various related crises and discovering the hidden resources in each other. A close family supported each other's strengths and discovered and accepted each other's dark sides and became even closer.

Add to that friends who over the years have become as close as family. Do you know that warm and fuzzy feeling when a friend unexpectedly arrives at the funeral of a person they did not know well and says 'Of course I was going to be here for you – what did you expect?'

 Have you been fortunate enough to get support from people you least expected it from? How did it impact on you

Today I am counting my blessings – and I will be very busy with that all day because there are so many.   And to think much of this happened because of the example set by one remarkable man that I could call my dad.

34 MURDER, YES. DIVORCE, NEVER

Picture this: Sicily 1965. (If you are giggling about this, you remember Sophia and you probably have grey hair!)

A couple has been married for 20 years. They have teenage children. He is the breadwinner – and he has done so well that his family now prefers the proverbial cake to bread. She is the home-maker – and she prefers to not leave home, in case a flower arrangement or a recipe needs urgent attention. The picture of perfection! Or is it?

Here is another picture: he started his career at a high, being the best student, then the best intern, then the heart and soul of the party and a social asset to the company – but not quite living up to professional expectations. She was the strong support in the background, and quietly worked her way out of the kitchen and onto the bench in the courtroom. They have a 'pigeon pair' son and daughter who are also achievers in their own right. Everything is all right – or is it?

In both instances the cracks in the marriage are there to see for everyone – except for the main players.

Too often couples achieve their 'picture of perfection' and are then trapped into maintaining their circumstances at all costs while they grow miles apart. And oh boy, do they pay – and pay.

Any change they are willing to accept must be external, as in a bigger house, a better car, more exotic holidays. The marriage must remain intact, 'until death us do part' – because that is the norm.

What are the consequences? The marriage becomes artificial. The participants become physically ill, because they resist change in their spirit, mind and body.

 Have you noticed a marriage that changed over time with the partners not noticing or accepting the changes in each other? What have you learnt from it?

Here are some tips on how to deal with the situation.

One: change happens all the time. Resist it at your peril, or ride the wave and grow from it.

☐ Two: A marriage certificate is a legal contract, not a death sentence. The contract is not a guarantee against change. The contract only spells out what the initial agreement was, and in some instances, it also documents the agreement on a potential outcome. The contract does not say that you will die if you are in breach. Experience says that you may die from ill health if you insist on never ending the contract and clinging to it at all costs. It's your call.

Three: There are two people in a marriage. They either grow together, or they grow apart. That is life. When you allow a whole community or society into the marriage, then nobody grows, except in terms of the amount of fear of change that they gather and share.

Every relationship has a natural life cycle. That includes a marriage. If people manage to let go of their fantasies and accept what comes natural, the end of a marriage will be accepted as a wonderful growth experience.

What we have instead is often a prolonged nightmare that is dictated to society by people who either vowed never to marry but made the rules, or who spend lots of energy upholding their own fantasy in the eyes of the world.

Here endeth the sermon.

Now get yourself a coach who understands that divorce is both the end of the world as you know it, and a tremendous opportunity for growth. Then find your own balance in your thinking, and get an amicable divorce where everyone can congratulate themselves on being better off emotionally and spiritually because of the divorce. Then get on with your life.

Or stay married and find yourself a good doctor who will help you camouflage all the symptoms of your distress, and spend all your energy on maintaining a fantasy in the eyes of the world, while you are deeply unhappy.

There is no reason to become a victim when your marriage ends.

I know which approach works – been there, done that, and lived to express my deep gratitude for the experience. I also learned how to cut the process of making sense out of the experience from 10 years to a few hours. It can be done because it is a scientific process that can be repeated at   will.

☐

35 DEALING WITH THE DEATH OF A PARTNER

When a person dies, we go through the stages of grieving. What is that grief, and what are we sad about?

 What are you sad about when a person dies? Why?

Assume that we do believe in eternal life. That means when a person dies, they leave their body behind and continue to live in a different form – a form that some of us recognize as the person's ethereal body. This happens because we are energy, and energy cannot be destroyed.

If the person continues to exist, but only in a different form, why do we get so sad about somebody dying? What exactly is it that we lose?

Death reminds us of our own mortality, and when we have unfinished business here, we feel pressure to get on with our own business. If we do not understand that we have all the time that is required to fulfill our purpose here, we will be sad.

Death also means that we will experience our relationship with the deceased person in a different way. We will no longer be able to talk to the person (or ignore the person if that is what we did when they were still alive). Thoughts of that person will fill our minds. Sometimes we will have loving conversations with the person, and at other times we will have nightmares about the person.

People come to this earth and inhabit their bodies because they have a purpose. They have specific lessons to learn, and to teach to others. All of us are here to learn and to teach.

When we no longer have anything to learn, the time comes when we leave our bodies behind. We can continue to teach others even after we had left our bodies. We do that by means of those conversations in our minds.

Once a person has left their body behind, they are in a state of Love, regardless of the nature of the earthly lives they had lived. That is why we have such loving experiences with our deceased loved ones.

But what if we have these nightmares and fears that continue after the person has passed on? If we do not understand this change, namely that the deceased person is in a state of Love, we continue to hold on to our own fears until we can resolve them.

Grieving is also about loss. We believe that once a person has passed on, we have lost everything we had with that person. We believe that we have lost a loving look, memories of good times together, and all the other things we wanted to hold on to.

This might sound strange, but death is not about loss, because we never lose anything. The Universe is in complete balance. We keep everything forever, and we need to find those things elsewhere. For example, after many years of marriage you lose the companionship of a loving partner. At the same time a friend supports you and a rich friendship takes the place of that companionship. Or you become more spiritually aware and continue the relationship with your partner, but in a spiritual way.

If death is not about loss, what is it about? Death is about re-assessing what we have, and about finding the balance again in a perfect Universe. The balance is there. When a person departs, we temporarily forget about the balance. We cry because we experience a sense of loss. Over time we regain our balance and we understand that we have lost nothing.

 Have you experienced a sense of loss from the death of a love one? What did you lose? What was the loss replaced with?

This applies to all losses and all grieving. Do you grieve about the loss of a friend? Did you because of the loss of the friendship gain new friends, which restored the balance? Do you grieve about the loss of a child? Have you, because of that, found other people to care for, maybe people who also lost children?

But some of you say 'no, this is not true for me. I have felt the pain of that loss and it will remain with me forever.' That is your choice. If you want to spend the rest of your life here cherishing the loss, you can do that. If you want to find out how the balance in your life has been restored, it will become clear to you very quickly.

When you are able and willing to understand what it is that you have lost and gained, you can move on and find that inner peace. When you choose to define yourself for the rest of your life in terms of your loss, the rest of your life will be off balance. The world will move on regardless of how you define yourself, and you are part of the world. Do you really want to live the rest of your life mourning something that you have not lost?

36 LETTING GO OF RESENTMENT

Love relationships can end in interesting ways, for example where ordinary people end an ordinary relationship, and then one person becomes famous. Suddenly the ex of an ordinary person becomes the forgotten past of a famous person.

Very few people in such a situation can actually walk away from the temptation to 'spill the beans'. And of course, the memories of the left-behind ordinary ex will be one-sided and not necessarily supported by the recollection of the famous ex.

Recently a well-known television figure was in the news because he had a gagging order on his ex-wife lifted. They were married for two years until the early nineties. A couple of years after their divorce he married his current wife. Now the ex-wife makes claims about a continued relationship with her after he re-married.

Whether her claims are true or not does not matter. What is important is that in a sense neither the man nor his ex-wife has left their relationship. They may have ended their physical relationship, but the emotional and spiritual relationship is still firmly in place, and both still need to work through their emotions resulting from that past relationship.

 Are you still at some level holding on to a past relationship? Why?

It would not be surprising if the ex-wife still has strong feelings of resentment about having left the relationship. The man really made his name on television after their marriage had ended, and the first wife was never part of the fame that he obtained while he was married to his second wife.

If the first wife could put the marriage behind her, she would have reached a point where she would be able to talk about her ex-husband with gratitude for what she gained from their relationship. Instead she loves to publicly go into detail about her reasons for ending their marriage, and how she was (and still is) affected by him.

What could she have gained from the relationship that she should be grateful for? Of course, their relationship has changed her for the better, and there is some wisdom that she has not acknowledged yet. Instead, she focuses on the destructive side of the relationship.

Has the man moved on? If he felt he needed a gagging order on his first wife nearly two decades later, then there are still some emotional buttons related to his relationship with his first wife that could be pressed. He needs to work through his emotions based on his relationship with her. It does not matter how long their physical relationship lasted. What matters is that he still has an emotional relationship with her, which will continue until he can look back at the experience with gratitude for having gained his own wisdom.

When the man can say 'It does not matter what she tells the world, because I have accepted my life and actions, learned from it and moved on', the emotional relationship between the two of them will finally come to an end.

As long as the man feels the need to defend himself against anything (whether it is true or false) from the past, he still has unresolved emotions that will result in a knee-jerk reaction every time a new 'revelation' is published.

Sadly, the press does not thrive on 'no comment'. If 'no comment' becomes his response to allegations because he has truly dealt with everything from the past, he may be found guilty by default. However, that will also be a test of whether he has truly put the relationship behind him or not.

Once both parties can be neutral and non-emotional about their past relationship, and once they can both express gratitude for what they have learnt about themselves from the relationship, the spiritual contract between them will come to an end. And that will truly be the end of the relationship.

37 GETTING DIVORCED – WITHOUT THE PAPERWORK

Does marriage happen in your heart or on paper?

A reality TV celebrity recently asked another reality TV star to marry him during a TV interview, and she accepted. Now he claims that 'in his heart' he is already married to his new fiancée, even though his marriage to his wife is still to be dissolved.

This situation seems to make a mockery of marriage – if you believe that marriage is 'until death us do part'. Like many other celebrities, this gentleman seems to move from one relationship to the next quite quickly, and one may jump to the conclusion that he does not understand the meaning of commitment and is therefore not relationship material.

However, his marriage and new relationship is a good example of the state of relationships, since we live in an age where relationships start and end much faster than in the past.

Every relationship has a natural end date. Yes, a relationship may be short-lived, like the two-year-marriage between this gentleman and his estranged wife - or it may last for 70 years, like the one between the couple who recently passed away within an hour of each other after both being injured in a car accident.

The question is not how long you can make a relationship or marriage last, but rather whether you can recognize the end of the relationship. Once it is clear that the relationship has come to an end and the partners still hold on, the situation normally becomes quite explosive. It becomes more and more difficult to move on and the emotions get stronger and more painful.

 In your experience, why would people hold on to a dreadfully unhappy relationship?

You know intuitively when you have reached the natural end of a relationship, because you start to withdraw physically and emotionally. Even if you yourself still feel committed, you will feel your partner withdraw and you will know that things are not the same any longer.

When you are married to your partner, there seems to be an obligation to do everything humanly possible to save the marriage, because if you do not stay married, you have failed. This attitude goes against nature, where everything happens in cycles – including relationships.

This gentleman seems on the surface to have recognized that his marriage relationship is truly over, and to have moved on. It is heartening news that he and his fiancée want to enjoy their engagement before they get married. That will give them both the time to deal with any final baggage from their past relationships.

And yes, dissolving his marriage to his estranged wife is part of moving on and it cannot be ignored. The legal process will still result in strong emotions related to the marriage that he must deal with, and those emotions will impact on his current relationship until he has dealt with them.

Will it be necessary for the gentleman and his fiancée to get married to prove their commitment to each other? That is a personal decision. He seems to understand from his own experience that a marriage certificate does not necessarily mean commitment to a person. He has already publicly declared his commitment to his fiancée and that is binding in his mind.

Will his commitment to his fiancée last forever? That depends entirely on the soul contract between them and the reason why they are having a relationship. Maybe it will, maybe it won't. Either way, if he and his fiancée ever part ways, it will mean the end of the relationship, and not the end of the world.

38 MARRYING INTO A DREAM

The TV star Kelsey Grammer once indicated in a TV interview that he thought his third wife married him because he was the very popular TV character, Frasier. She married her dream, and the reality turned out to be an ordinary, vulnerable person with extra-ordinary talents.

Did the same happen when the model Heather Mills married the musician Paul McCartney? Did she also marry a dream and wake up to a different reality?

This does not only happen to rich and famous people. Women often get married to a 'knight in shining armor' who takes them away from circumstances that they dislike – only to find that the truth is not in the new circumstances, but in how they view their lives.

For example, a teenage girl married a man who took her away from parents that relied financially on their child, and she had big dreams of a life of being in the limelight. A month after the marriage she found herself pregnant in a culture where abortion was not an option, and where everyone celebrated the arrival of an heir. She discovered that she had moved from an escapable nightmare to an inescapable nightmare, and she was forced into the role of mother prematurely – with disastrous consequences. She eventually died from an overdose of drugs because she could not cope with her life-long devils and disillusionment.

Do you know anyone who married for the wrong reasons?
How do you know the reasons were wrong?

We like to read in the press about well-known people having whirlwind romances and getting married quickly. However, we are left with a sense of confusion when those fairy-tale romances disintegrate into bitter public divorces.

How can such an outcome be prevented for an ideal courtship?

The Universe is in complete balance – for every action there is an equal and opposite reaction, as Isaac Newton discovered centuries ago. This has in recent decades been confirmed when it was discovered that every positive charge also has a negative charge.

Where a famous (or not so famous) person is swept away into a wonderful romance, and there is talk of marriage or even living together as an indication of commitment, the couple should be encouraged to take stock of their situation. They should be guided to discover the downside of every dream-like experience that they have together.

And no, this is not the opposite of positive thinking. This is a means of finding balance. If the focus is entirely on the dream-like experiences, the laws of nature will ensure that the nightmare-like side of the experience will be added. Why not rather find the balance before making a public commitment that could result in an equally public down-fall?

For example, when you marry a famous person, you get famous by default for a short time. However, over time the famous, talented person continues to get the attention based on their talents, while the not-so-famous spouse fades into the background.

Even when you marry a person who is successful but not famous, you may find that their success is based on a single-mindedness that excludes everything else while they pursue their dream. And what if you are part of that dream, and you lose their interest once they have 'achieved' you?

Look for the downside of your dream before you leap. That will help you to find balance and make more realistic decisions.

39 CAN YOU TRUST YOUR INTUITION IN A RELATIONSHIP?

A reality show star married a professional basketball player after a whirl-wind romance, and decided to divorce him after just 72 days of marriage based on 'irreconcilable differences'.

When questioned on a breakfast show about her decision to get a divorce, she apparently answered: 'I think when you know so deep in your heart that you just listen to your intuition and follow your heart, there's no right or wrong thing to do.'

This begs the question: did she follow her intuition when she decided to get married, or did she ignore her intuition at that point and only chose to follow her heart after the marriage hype, when reality settled in?

It is quite possible that she did both. Even the most intuitive people make decisions that take them into difficult times, only to have to recover later and move on. This is not just human folly - it is the pattern of life.

The whole purpose of our lives is to have various experiences that challenge us and break down pre-conceived ideas, so that we can grow and learn.

More intuitive people know that when these significant life experiences happen, their intuition takes a back-seat. At the time, it is quite frustrating, because you want to find an easy way out of the situation. You know that your intuition will always show you the least painful option, and it can be quite challenging to discover that you cannot find an intuitive solution to your situation.

However, once you have resolved the life lesson and you are ready to move on, your intuition returns – and it is even stronger than it has ever been before.

It is quite possible that this lady did not follow her intuition when she decided to get married, but that she did follow her intuition in deciding to get divorced. It is also possible that she is not really intuitive, and that she does not yet realize the nature of the wisdom that she needs to discover from her decisions.

Either way, she did remind us that it is important to be aware of our intuition and follow our hearts.

 Have you ever ignored your intuition and made a decision that you later regretted?

40 MOVING ON FROM THE WRONG RELATIONSHIP

How is it that some people feel their lives stopped when they married someone?

It is interesting how, in some relationships, we grow emotionally and spiritually as part of the relationship, while in other relationships our lives are placed on hold and we only experience pain as part of the relationship

Why is it that we decide to enter some relationships, while we intuitively know that we are doing the wrong thing? This could relate to both a love, work or friendship relationship. In the moment that we make the decision we know it is the wrong decision. However, we seem to go on auto pilot and stay on this destructive path.

Often the decision has other consequences, for example you know that you are married to the wrong person, you know that you need to end the relationship at the first opportunity, but nevertheless you continue and for example have a child with this person. You justify the situation in every way you can think of, and finally the pain of staying where you are becomes greater than moving on.

Only at that point do you gather the courage to take that step out of the relationship.

Then why did you enter the relationship in the first place? Because you had a soul contract with the other person. As part of your destiny you needed to honor the contract.

What is the nature and purpose of the soul contract?

 Do you have a soul contract with anyone? What is the nature of the soul contract?

That differs from one relationship to the next. In some instances, the

purpose is to deal with physical or emotional violence and find your own inner strength that you otherwise would not be aware of. In other instances, the purpose would be to discover your power to control your own life, and to take the control from the person you married and get your own life on track again.

Or you could for example need to experience emotional coldness from your partner so that you can understand the importance of acknowledging and dealing with your own emotions.

Where children are involved, part of your soul contract is to raise and nurture the child, because that child chose you and your partner as their parents. The child also chose emotional and spiritual experiences as part of their life path, and you and your partner represent those experiences.

Either way, at some point that soul contract between you and your partner comes to a natural end. When that happens, you find the strength to walk away from the relationship.

Does this mean the end of the relationship? No. Yes, you do realize that you have placed a large part of your life on hold, and you suddenly have the energy and inclination to continue with activities that you had left behind at the beginning of the destructive relationship.

However, this is only the beginning of the resumed personal growth. You truly get back on track when you look back at the relationship and discover the wisdom that you were meant to discover in the process.

Look back at the blessings from the relationship, for example your children, knowing how wrong it is to marry for pity rather than love, understanding the importance of listening to your intuition, finding your own power and using that to build your ideal future for yourself.

When you are ready to leave the relationship, you will discover how help comes your way in many forms – from physical help in moving house to making new friends that help you feel comfortable being your new self, to support from your children who want to see you happy and intuitively have a better grasp on the situation that you often give them credit for.

The first step is to stop castigating yourself for making a 'wrong' decision and look for the wisdom and the blessings. The rest will follow naturally.

ABOUT THE AUTHOR

Elsabe Smit is a well-known international coach, facilitator, author, and public speaker that uses her clairvoyant and intuitive skills in her daily life to assist all of those that she comes into contact with in her professional life.

She has an MBA (Master Business Administration), a MA in Industrial Psychology, and extensive experience as a Business Analyst. Using all her knowledge, skills and competencies, Elsabe helps people to understand the mysteries of life and Love, so that they can regain control of their lives.

Elsabe Smit was born and raised in South Africa, but has since 2000 been living in the UK.

After years of facing numerous personal challenges, involving her relationship with her drug- and alcohol-addicted mother, living with and getting divorced from an abusive husband, being a single mother, being a mistress for a period, and then facing unemployment, she one day realized that she had been given the amazing gift of intuition and clairvoyance.

Using her newly discovered gifts, she then rediscovered herself. She learned that all her past experiences, "good" and "bad", were only stepping stones on her life's blueprint towards loving and accepting herself.

Having always having had a keen interest in human behavior, this discovery took her on a different path, adding the study of life, death and spirituality to her interests. During that journey, she explored NLP and embraced Quantum Physics. Elsabe studied some of the world's best acknowledged researchers and gurus in the fields of relationships, health and business.

During her professional life, Elsabe's career included lecturing at a South African University, being a Human Resources Manager with a mining house and a multinational security firm, and being a freelance business analyst.

In between the various permanent positions and contracts, she developed her reputation as a sought-after author, speaker, facilitator, coach and mentor.

As an author, some of her books are today still in use as prescribed text books for university and college students in South Africa. Other books have been published and are available on Amazon, and some books have been published as E-books which she shares as free gifts.

As a speaker, facilitator and trainer she has presented numerous programmes to groups ranging from a dozen to hundreds of people. The subject matter has been as varied and interesting as her life.

As a mentor, she coached and mentored small business owners, blue-chip executives and employees covering a myriad of professions, employment levels and industries.

Don't forget her contribution to the world of psychics. She's been on various radio and TV shows with international audiences. In addition, Elsabe has done thousands of personal psychic readings for people from all walks of life located in more than 80 countries - including one for a death row inmate in a US prison.

Throughout her life, Elsabe has been passionately focused on identifying the nuances that make a difference in people lives, the why's of birth, life and death - and now it's your turn to tap into the vast wealth of knowledge and experiences that she has gained during her lifetime, so that like Elsabe ...

YOU can also Discover yourself and Love YOUR Life.

If you have questions, or comments, contact Elsabe at elsabe@elsabesmit.com, or visit her website at www.elsabesmit.com to access her skill so that you can resolve your burning issue.

You can also follow Elsabe on
`Twitter (https://twitter.com/ElsabeSmit)
LinkedIn (http://www.linkedin.com/in/elsabesmit)
YouTube (https://www.youtube.com/user/ElsabeSmit)
   Google+ (https://plus.google.com/+ElsabeSmit/posts)

MORE FROM THIS AUTHOR

Are you stuck in a relationship that has reached a dead end?

Is a past relationship still haunting you?

Then you have come to the right place!

This book will quickly give you a new perspective and help you to move on and have a happy life. The book will show you how your current or past partner has helped you learn about yourself. You will recover from any relationship and feel very good about yourself.

Make a small investment in your future happiness, and you will receive answers and solutions that will make your heart sing again.

Here is what the book can do for you:

- Help you understand the purpose of your relationship.
- Explain how your partner thinks.
- Define true Love and why it is so elusive.
- Find your motive for staying in a destructive relationship
- Provide a step by step solution for ending the relationship.
- Take away your guilt and resentment.
- Help you discover the value in any relationship - even a bad one.
- Stop those nightmares and sleepless nights.
- Explain why it is OK for your relationship to end.
- Discover why you have stayed in a destructive relationship until now.

- Explain the true meaning of gratitude.
- Discover how gratitude releases you from your relationship.
- Give you a vision of your future.
- Show you how to find the strength to move on.
- Teach you to Love the face in your mirror again.

This is what readers have said about the book:

"You can feel the compassion in her words, how awesome is that. Thank you so much for such a wonderful, positive response."

"Thank you so much for the help, my dear friend. I could say thanks you a million times or at least in several different languages but it still wouldn't get the point across. Thank you."

"That makes a lot of sense. I'm going to sit down and talk with him tonight and see where we stand as for the wedding. I love him and we'll make it work no matter what. Thanks."

"Makes perfect sense!"

"Recently I have had Elsabe's wisdom and experience on ending a relationship. I must admit I have never ended a relationship without feeling guilt, remorse or a sense of devastation, but this time Elsabe helped me to see that the relationship had come to its natural end and I was able to let go and move on with love in my heart for my ex-partner and no feeling of having to make amends or justify my actions. My ex-partner has let me go too. WE came to a mutual understanding that we had some wonderful times together and that we had both seen positive changes happen in each other over the years we were together. Elsabe has helped me accept that relationships don't last forever and once we they have served their purpose there is only pain if we chose to hang on to them 'past their sell by date'. I feel remarkably different now like a weight has been lifted. Thank you, Elsabe, for your valuable time wisdom and insight. Your message is one which I know others will be blessed to hear."

Search for the book on your local Amazon website, or contact the author on www.ElsabeSmit.com to order a signed copy.

Have you always wanted to understand how energy healing works?

Is energy healing the placebo effect in a different form?

This book conveys a powerful promise early on and then delivers on this promise throughout the material:

"Every physical illness and dis-ease stems from a disturbance in the rhythm of time. We will go back to the disturbance and allow time to flow freely. This will then remove the energy block and this is where the healing takes place."

The book gives a different perspective on the age-old question of why God allows suffering and claims to be a God of Love:

"God only creates that which is beyond time and space. People then distil from God's creation and add their own details, and they fall back on their indoctrination to pass the credit as well as the blame for the creation of their own making on to God."

This book explains how healing empowers people:

"...people get an understanding of their own creative powers. They understand that they have created the dis-ease. They understand that they create the cure. They understand the difference between their own creative powers and the creative powers of God. Most important, they gain an understanding of a loving God."

Healing is explained as undoing the behavior that caused the dis-ease, then undoing the dis-ease, and then re-doing the behavior without the dis-ease, so that the person can consciously change their behavior and not fall back into the toxic patterns that resulted from the original injury.

The author of the book warns that energy healing is not necessarily about extending this physical life:

"At all times the focus of healing is to remove the energy blockage and to provide a belief system that will allow the person to continue on the journey."

This healing is truly holistic.

"We do not just heal the symptoms, because when we do that, the behavior pattern will remain and the damage will be repeated, often on an even larger scale. We remove the energy blockage, and at the same time we do deep healing work on the spirit."

There are several powerful comments that shed a new light on beliefs and physical conditions e.g. obesity:

"The whole purpose of religion is to make people weak and to ensure that they are malleable, in other words to suck out their energy and replace it with a Void that they feel as long as they are in the power of religion. Obese people fill that Void with food and drink."

There is a lot more in this book than just the extracts above.

Search for the book on your local Amazon website, or contact the author on www.ElsabeSmit.com to order a signed copy.

In this enlightening book, internationally renowned psychic, coach and author Elsabe Smit breaks down some key concepts of spiritual development into short, highly accessible articles, and provides ways in which the reader can achieve spiritual growth.

Inspired by a lifetime of facing sometimes seemingly insurmountable challenges, Elsabe examines the subtle nuances that influence our lives, and explores these age-old questions: Why are we born? How can we get closer to enlightenment? Is there life after death?

Drawing on elements of quantum physics, plus works by some of the world's most prominent researchers and gurus in the fields of health, business and relationships, Elsabe will help you to understand the ancient mystery of Love.

She will help you to regain control of your life and, using spiritual concepts, find enlightenment in life's daily challenges.

All life experiences, whether you label them as 'good' or 'bad', are simply stepping stones on a journey towards finding self-acceptance, compassion and your own spirituality.

In this highly practical guide to modern day spirituality, Elsabe shares her life experiences and wealth of knowledge gained over many years both on this plane and in psychic work.

Elsabe will show you how to discover your true self and to appreciate the life you have been given.

In "*Spiritual Growth: How to Strengthen Your Faith and Spirituality (The Enlightenment Series Volume 1)*" you will get answers to these questions:

- Where do I find solace?

- How can I improve my karma?
- Why do we experience the dark night of the soul and how can we get through it?
- How do we match our expectations to the outcomes we get?
- What is the true meaning of time and numbers?
- Does faith require trust and belief?
- How do the risks we take strengthen our faith?
- How do you celebrate your beliefs?
- Did you know that clinging to the wrong idea can affect your health?
- Why is it important to live every day, not just Sundays, as part of your faith?
- How can the Law of Attraction give you the opposite of what you want?
- How do you have to explore your Awareness and find your spiritual teacher?
- How do you deal with tough decisions about injustice to others?
- How to practice detachment and improve your own judgement
- How to find the gain from dealing with grief and death
- How to identify and eliminate your self-imposed labels and boundaries
- Why should older people be respected?
- Who is your neighbour and how should you love your neighbour?
- How can you deal with prejudice?
- Why does the church discriminate against gay people and females?

The book is written as a series of short articles with useful prompts throughout that encourage you to pause and reflect, make notes, answer questions and complete exercises.

Search for the book on your local Amazon website, or contact the author on www.ElsabeSmit.com to order a signed copy.

In this enlightening book, internationally renowned psychic and author Elsabe Smit breaks down some key concepts of spiritual development into short, highly accessible articles, and provides ways in which you can find spiritual meaning in your daily life. She questions mundane experiences and finds the practical meaning of spirit in this age of enlightenment.

All experiences, whether you label them as 'good' or 'bad', are simply stepping stones on a journey towards finding self-acceptance and compassion in this age of enlightenment.

Elsabe will show you how to discover spiritual meaning and appreciate your life.

In *"More of Life's Questions: Find Your Moment of Revelation (The Enlightenment Series Vol 3)"* you will find enlightenment and define your own spirituality with these questions:

How to respect religion and religious boundaries even if you are not religious

How the flow of energy impacts on our relationships

How we set boundaries for ourselves and delay our own enlightenment experiences

How the creation process works and how we can use that to find spiritual meaning

How to find your way through life with pen and paper rather than expensive therapy by using the most potent journaling method known.

And many other questions.

The book is written as a series of short articles with useful prompts throughout that encourage you to pause and reflect, make notes, answer questions and complete exercises. By the end of this book you will define spirituality in your own way an understand what enlightenment is about.

Search for the book on your local Amazon website, or contact the author on www.ElsabeSmit.com to order a signed copy.

Inspirational daily quotes for each day of the year to encourage spiritual growth and explain why certain events happen in your life

Ask yourself the following:

- Do you notice the small miracles in your life?
- Do you see the truth in mundane events?
- Do you like to start your day with a spiritual pick-me-up?

If you answered YES to the above, then this book is for you.

Elsabe Smit has a knack for bringing spiritual teaching into our lives by interpreting events. She sees the truth in small things and brings them in line with the spiritual teachings that are sometimes hard to put into practice.

In this book, she shares her wisdom in a simple, effective way by providing snippets for contemplation.

In *"Wonder Why? Inspirational Daily Quotes for All Ages"* you will learn:

- How your perceptions influence your experience
- Why having strong emotions about anything makes your life worse
- How to use humor that bites like a lamb rather than a lion
- That under the skin we all share the same life experiences
- How tradition sometimes is based on wrong information
- Why carrying grudges is not healthy
- That life and the Universe aims at helping us find balance
- What energy is and how to use energy
- How to get the best out of change
- How to turn incidents into opportunities

And many other themes …

The book is written as a series of inspirational daily quotes on which you can pause and reflect every day.

Search for the book on your local Amazon website, or contact the author on www.ElsabeSmit.com to order a signed copy.

If you discovered this book because you were looking for chocolate recipes, then there was some divine intervention.

It is possible that your soul is starving for some inspiring, non-fattening soul chocolate.

Dip into this book daily to get some inspiration and sustenance, and help you focus on your own truth. Find meaning in simple things and add soul music to your life.

All you need to do is open this book on any page, and you have a focus for your **daily meditation**, providing **sustenance for your soul**.

Search for the book on your local Amazon website, or contact the author on www.ElsabeSmit.com to order a signed copy.

Have you ever experienced a definitive moment that shaped your life and determined your future?

Have you observed the actions of a loved one and asked yourself why they acted as they did?

Did you ever experience a true light-bulb moment that has stayed with you ever since?

Do you sometimes feel as if you are the only person on this planet who had a mind-blowing experience?

Or do you like to read about the lives of other people to help you make sense of your own experiences?

Then this book is for you.

The book contains short inspirational stories about life. Each story deals with a different theme, indicating the motivation behind the actions of the people involved, and how they were inspired in various ways, for example insights into their choices that brought them peace of mind, or a moment of inspiration after having an out-of-this-world experience.

The stories make you think about your own situation and how you can be inspired to new insights.

Search for the book on your local Amazon website, or contact the author on www.ElsabeSmit.com to order a signed copy.

How do you manage to stay afloat and keep your faith or moral compass in a changing world? How do you find direction when everyone else is panicking and the changes become too big to understand?

This channeled book adds new meaning to our existence, and provides clear guidelines on how to create order from chaos by having a different view of the world.

The book provides gems such as

- What energy is and how to use energy in the creative process
- How to understand and benefit from the nature of time
- What forgiveness really means
- The importance of water not only for cleansing, but as a messenger
- Explaining the meaning of eternity and where we fit into eternity
- The true nature of faith and what to do when your faith dries up
- How to create abundance
- A view of the emerging world and a roadmap for navigating new challenges in this world

Psychic and author Elsabe Smit received these messages of assurance and explanation from the Pleiades and is finally sharing them with those who are ready to listen and act.

Search for the book on your local Amazon website, or contact the author on www.ElsabeSmit.com to order a signed copy.

RESILIENCE

How to conquer the
fear and challenges
of self-employment

Fraser J. Hay   Elsabe Smit

If you would like to experience the practical application of Elsabe's wisdom, get yourself a copy of the book *"Resilience: How to Conquer the Fears and Challenges of Self-Employment."*

Self-Employed? Ever felt frustrated, isolated - even desperate on occasion with no-one to turn to for help, guidance or support? If so, then this powerful, practical book will help you to keep moving forwards and living your dream.

Ask yourself the following questions:

- How do you take your business from brain to heart to stellar?
- Where does forgiveness feature in your business plan?
- Why do bad things happen to good people, despite their best intentions?
- What if the business idea you have put your heart and soul into goes wrong?
- Who do you turn to for advice and how can you keep on track in the face of adversity?

The powerful, proven, practical and highly effective concepts, techniques, and spiritual principles in this book can be applied to almost every commercial problem, issue or challenge that you will face in starting and running your own business.

Real world, practical examples and exercises are included for you to personalize and apply to your current circumstances.

Ever been anxious, frustrated or worried about:

- What makes you really "different" or unique in your marketplace?
- Deciding and accepting what you really offer potential customers?
- Finding, winning and keeping Customers?
- Charging (and getting paid) what you're really worth?
- Juggling home life with running a business?
- Making the right decision at the right time?
- Getting paid for work already done?
- Personal and professional conflict?
- Allowing your fears to prevent you from achieving your goals?
- Dealing with the emotional stress of starting and running your own business?
- Learning to know, like and trust yourself?

"Resilience: How to Conquer the Fears and Challenges of Self-Employment" shares a common-sense approach that simply isn't common practice among the millions of self-employed facing the daily issues, challenges & obstacles of self-employment that are holding them back and preventing them from achieving their personal, professional and commercial goals and objectives.

Discover:

- How to make sense of conflict - since you cannot avoid it
- How to turn rejection into opportunity
- When do you celebrate success and when to navigate hurdles for even greater success
- Where to find inspired answers and solutions
- How you can prepare for meetings knowing the outcome in advance
- When to walk away and when to fight back, and why
- What the real "lessons" are that you need to master, to guarantee your personal success
- How to reassure yourself, your family or your loved ones that you're mentally prepared for the challenges presented to you, your finances or your health

You want to work for yourself and you want to be in control of your own destiny. We know it, you know it and your heart knows it! Do you want to live the life and lifestyle you've always craved?

You've already got the power and resilience to succeed in self-employment.

You just need to recognize it, and be shown how to use it.

Search for the book on your local Amazon website, or contact the author on www.ElsabeSmit.com to order a signed copy.

ONE LAST THING ...

If you believe the book is worth sharing, please would you take a few seconds to leave a review on Amazon and let your friends know about it? If it turns out to make a difference in their lives, they'll be forever grateful to you, as will I.

www.ingramcontent.com/pod-product-compliance
Lightning Source LLC
Chambersburg PA
CBHW072025290526
45787CB00015B/2038